People's Park
Still Blooming
1969-2009 and on...
Edited by Terri Compost

www.peoplespark.org

First Edition 2009
Published by Slingshot Collective,
a project of Long Haul, Inc.
3124 Shattuck Ave.
Berkeley, CA 94705
http://slingshot.tao.ca
510 540-0751

Copyright 2009
All rights reserved
with original sources

ISBN # 978-0-9841208-0-2
Library of Congress Control Number: 2009906332

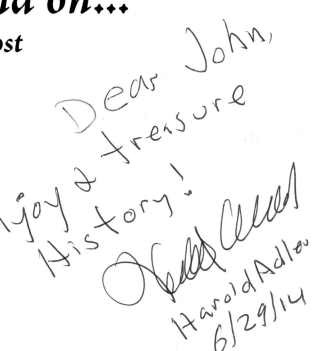

Dear John, enjoy & treasure History! [signature] Harold Adler 6/29/14

Printed in the USA
Sheridan Books, Inc.
Ann Arbor, MI 48103
www.sheridanbooks.com

Front cover National Guard photo: *Bill Haigwood, 1969*
Back cover: National Guard photo: *Kenneth Green, "Azalea",*
May 18, 1969. The Oakland Tribune Collection, the Oakland
Museum of California. Gift of ANG Newspapers.
Woman planting photo: *John Jekabson, 1969*

This book is dedicated to Tristan Anderson
for his acts of courage and love
and for his healing.

Table of Contents

Preface and Introduction   v
Timeline   viii
Thanks   x

People's Park Today   1

Before the Park   6
   Abuse of Eminent Domain

Creation: A Thousand Blisters and a Dream   10

Paradise Lost: Authorities React   18
   The Fence   19
   Battle in the Streets   22
   Occupation   27
   Memorial Day March   33

Resistance and Hope   35
   The Fence Comes Down
   Garden Again   36
   Parking Lot to Garden 1979   37

Volleyballed: Eight police departments   40
       to build a volleyball court?
   Slapp Suit   60
   Rosebud Murdered   61

Commonland   62

Community Garden   67

User Development   79
   Work Parties   81
   Art   86

Sharing   91
   Clothes Freebox   92
   Sharing Food   95
   Refuge   99
   Survival Under Capitalism   100
   Social Activism   103
   Free Speech   108

Celebrations   115

Community   132

University of California   150

Memorials   156

Let 1000 Parks Bloom   164

Over the Years   167

Visions   177

People   181

Bibliography   189

Do It Yourself Gardens and Parks   190

Preface

This book celebrates 40 years since the creation of People's Park. People's Park — depending on your mood or whom you ask — is a 2.8 acre public park covered with trees and grass located between Haste Street and Dwight Way a half-block East of Telegraph Avenue in Berkeley, California. Or the park is a historical landmark — a symbol of all the political and cultural struggles of the 1960s. Or, the park is a problem, visited by too many homeless people.

People's Park is famous and controversial because of its dramatic creation story. In 1969, a diverse spontaneous coalition of radicals, visionaries and ordinary Berkeley people gathered to build the park themselves, on land they knew they didn't own, without seeking permission and without any formal planning. The action was provocative and radical but also peaceful, hopeful and simple. Building the park was a kind of protest without signs. Rather than beg for a new world based on less materialistic, more sustainable, more democratic values, people built a park that was the living embodiment of their dreams and alternative values.

The University of California, Berkeley (UC) — which (disputably) legally owned the land and which had been fighting increasingly bitter skirmishes with radicals and the counter-culture in Berkeley for years during the 1960s — responded ferociously to construction of the park. After thousands labored over a period of weeks to build a park, police seized it back in an early morning raid, leading to days of violent protests. Alameda County Sheriffs fired live ammunition into crowds, killing James Rector and wounding many others. The National Guard occupied Berkeley. This violent, authoritarian over-reaction may have done more to guarantee the park's continued survival than anything activists could have organized. The park became sacred ground —the University's land title forever stained with blood.

This book seeks to go beyond the creation story which has already been told, re-told, analyzed, celebrated and questioned many times over the last 40 years. The Park is more than a historical landmark or relic recalling the struggles of the 1960s — it is a physical place that exists day-to-day now, in 2009. This book comes out of the community around the park now — composed of people who mostly weren't involved in the struggles of the 1960s. While we often feel inspired by those struggles and the vision for a new kind of park and a new kind of world they embody, we and the park can't be limited to an echo from the past.

A key to understanding how the park has evolved over the last 40 years — and perhaps the key message this book might impart to readers — is the concept of User Development. User Development means that the people who use a particular space like the park should be the ones who determine how it is developed and operated. User Development applies the idea of direct democracy championed by New Left groups from the 1960s like Students for a Democratic Society. Hierarchical social structures like the university bureaucracy in 1969 couldn't permit people to build a park without studies, permits, experts or budgets because to do so would demonstrate that hierarchy isn't necessary for humans to live on the earth. Permitting User Development would show that people can do stuff for themselves. Almost all the battles fought over People's Park since 1969 have involved the collision between People's Park users' desire to develop the park as they saw fit versus the university's desire to exert top-down control. University bureaucrats who seek to control what happens at the park rarely actually use the park.

The struggles over the park have been a microcosm of larger social struggles. Are people part of nature, or should human societies dominate nature? Should private property rights or human use value be prioritized? How should democracy be practiced and where are people free to speak and assemble? How should a rich society deal with its poor and homeless people? How much should UC dominate the city of Berkeley?

But the park has always been more than a symbol in these struggles. People have fought to express alternative visions and forms of social organization in the real world — in a real physical park. As this book is published, the park is still a living struggle. Perhaps people who read this book will be inspired to create their own physical expressions of their dreams for a different world — be they parks or new types of workplaces, living groups, relationships or schools.

We have not always succeeded in our efforts to transform the world, and the park often reflects and emphasizes these failures. The park needs a book on its 40th anniversary and it needs constant struggle and effort precisely because the park is an imperfect experiment.

The typical anti-park rhetoric — that the park is too dangerous to visit, a source of criminal and drug activity in Berkeley, dirty and un-usable by anyone who is housed or middle class — is decidedly false. As demonstrated by this book, the park is used by a wide variety of people for a wide variety of purposes. On an average day, it is crowded with people. Surely that is an important measure of a successful park — that it is enjoyed by a lot of people.

But it is correct that the park is heavily used by homeless and non-mainstream people — some younger, some older, many unusual looking or scraggly. Sometimes people yell or mutter to themselves. Sometimes people are drunk or on drugs or act aggressively for their own reasons. Other times, the park feels mellow and innocent. Free food is served almost daily, attracting more people who need free food than people who don't need free food.

Part of the point of this book is to make clear that the park is highly diverse — it is not used solely by the homeless. But it's also important to keep in mind that the homeless are just people — the same as people who are housed or have more resources. They are not garbage; they are human beings. You cannot "clean up the park" by getting rid of the homeless. Perhaps if society is horrified seeing homeless or crazy people, our culture should work for more equality and a way of life that doesn't drive so many of us crazy.

The park has more than its share of homeless people not because there is something wrong with the park, but because these people are excluded and driven away from almost every other place in the urban environment. Most of the city-scape is designed for materialism and closed if you can't afford to consume. The park is unique in that it is open to everyone — a significant daily victory. In a society where few places are open to everyone, any place that is open to all will see a heavier concentration of people who are cast-off. Openness to all is a hopeful, utopian goal worth struggling for. It is sad that some people won't visit the park because they don't feel comfortable around marginalized people.

An important question is what could the park have become if the university hadn't fought park users' efforts to improve the park every step of the way? So much has been spent on police, bulldozers, fences, and jails. There's no way to tell, and no way to tell whether the university has learned from the past, or whether they'll spend the next 40 years using more police to try to beat down the park and its users day-to-day.

Often it seems UC wants the park to fail — or at least be perceived as a failure — so they can justify taking it back. Just as the park is sacred to some of its users because of the historical circumstances of its creation, the park is a continuing reminder to UC of its brutality. UC has played a two-faced game: pitting community members against each other by stopping improvements in the park while complaining that the park should be improved. Park supporters have frequently been on the defensive, outspent and subject to police attack.

When UC tried to build the volleyball courts in 1991, they figured enough time had passed so that they could finally take back the park. But for 40 years, attacking the park has awakened a sleeping bull and brought chaos to the streets. Because the park is constantly recruiting youthful dreamers who make the park their own, the university will never be able to take back the park because the park will never be merely a relic or a memory.

This book may be confusing in places because it features quotes from all sides — people who love the park and those who hate it. The park's story is one of constant conflict and struggle. If everyone agreed on what the park means and what should happen there, you wouldn't need a whole book to understand the last 40 years.

When the park was born, its creators were radicals seeking to create a new world. After 40 years of struggle with an imperfect park to show for it, are park supporters now the real conservatives, clinging to old tired visions and a tarnished dream? No. The park still represents a radical vision of user development and non-materialistic values that prioritize cooperation, sharing, ecological sustainability and people over profits. Sometimes the park is a mess, but it is our mess — something we have truly built ourselves despite constant UC attempts to stop us. It has been won with our blood and sweat.

So many people have been inspired to work hard to make the park what it is today because we are so desperately in need of meaningful alternatives to the mainstream culture of consumerism, pollution and powerlessness. May this book inspire you to create your own alternatives full of beauty, engagement and freedom.

— Jesse D. Palmer
Written in People's Park,
March 26, 2009

Introduction
Still the Vision Lingers On...

I hope that, like seeds, copies of this book will find fertile ground in the hearts of young people and will help them know the past...and encourage them to try again. We are connected. The land wants to live. Let a thousand parks bloom.

Tilling the soil of People's Park, I have found something precious ...alive. It is not healthy and thriving. It is worn and tired, desperate, and in danger. Fed on kindness and sharing and persistence, this little light flickers in a cement capitalist world, in the shadow of a corporate university so cut off from life that it mechanically destroys it. People's Park exposes this.

And the Park, as it was at its birth, remains an antidote. The Park turns the mad race for money on its head and relies on an economy of sharing. It brings people together in place and equality. It shows us the way to bring back nature to land that was built over. It teaches us how to get along with others. It reconnects us with soil and life and the sacredness of the land. It reminds us of the importance of history and our roles in it. It offers blossoms and birds, mud and softness to our poor city souls. It gives us sustenance and purpose, a chance to make a difference, a chance to help, a place to sing and dance. It is our victory, tattered as it is.

This book is for those that hear the name "People's Park", like I did, and know deep down that it is theirs and something to defend. And create. May you know more of our story, the humor and beauty, the struggle that so many have been part of. So much is changing so quickly, I cannot know what will be saved, but here is my prayer that the meaning of People's Park will continue to inspire.

—Terri

♦♦♦

Why have I fallen in love with People's Park? I learned of "the sixties" in a freshman english course in 1981, as an historian, uncovering a past time, so recent, yet hidden from me in a society doing its best at being recovered from such times. Perhaps because I'm a hippie at heart, I yearned for those dreams,

cherished the music and stumbled my way to the remnants still visible; Grateful Dead Shows, The Rainbow Gatherings and People's Park. I have not been disappointed by what I have found. The authenticity, though tattered is fresh air in a conditioned society. Many "hippies" did not "sell out" but have gone on living incredible and creative lives, and are inspiring elders now.

What have we learned? Where are we now? Dare I still dream that if I keep composting, nurturing the dreams—they will grow again? And somehow we will be able to aikido the violence because our need to evolve will open us to recognize, we are all in this together. How can we not try?

This book is not a comprehensive history of the last 40 years of People's Park. It is instead an attempt to capture the spirit and story of the Park. My own understanding of People's Park greatly changed when, at the Ashby Flea Market, I noticed a cut up copy of "People's Park", Alan Copeland and Nikki Arai's 1969 collection of photos. That book came out when the Park was fenced and the story seemed over. But it wasn't. The spirit has lived on in the struggle for this land. Here is the sequel.

❖❖❖

This is our valuable family heirloom, our memories, scrapbook, story of the courage and hope that freed and tended this sacred piece of earth. It is for us to remember, but mostly it is for the next to come.

This small piece of land holds a big story; of creation and loss, cooperation and reclaiming, neglect and decay, celebration and persistence, but mostly of the sharing of common land. Born in struggle in 1969, People's Park is a tale of people uniting to stand up to injustice. There are many people's dreams, sweat and tears nourishing the soil of today's humble appearing Park.

The Park is alive. It did and does embody the hopes of the sixties, and more. It also carries the scars and awkwardness of her brutal repression as she came to bloom. She hides the shame of the father, misunderstanding his child and worse reacting with violence to her freedom and beauty. How much was lost? Could it have been otherwise?

And yet miracle, she IS still. And beautiful to me. And to many. Wretched, frightening, disgusting to others. What does she still tell and ask of us? Here she is with her failures and lack of becoming, her hope and incredible beauty, a place where miracles happen.

People's Park is such a trouble maker. And it attracts such, a cast of characters. It remains free. Liberated by stubbornness, love, work and rebellion. So many claim her, people with not much to lose, people who still believe, people who need people and freedom and wildness. There is truth here. The pulse of American travelers is measured on her skin. The health of society, the creativity of resistance, the hope of the people are all played out on her soil. The web of people that remember, care and act for People's Park is tentative and fragile. There is such chaos in our lives: refugees, activists, dreamers, outcasts, survivors, those who think for ourselves, and try to be free in a controlled society, meeting in our sacred refuge to hold hands and know that community, land, hope, sharing . . . are here in our hands. Acts of obstinance and generosity, need, hope, loneliness, desire, but acts for the commons.

The web is fragile and yet the park has such deep roots and strong ghosts. They rise up to give us strength and righteousness. They call out supporters hidden in fabric of a society that seems to have forgotten. They link us with a larger struggle and remind us of the potency of symbolism. The park is rebellious by nature. It comes to life when threatened. It doesn't behave.

❖❖❖

The moment of history in which we celebrate the 40th anniversary of the creation of the park feels like a precipice. Berkeley, the country, humanity and nature are all falling into something else. Trying to hold onto what is alive. As I write this, the University has plans to build a bunch of creepy evil labs up our precious Strawberry Creek Canyon in Berkeley . . . and what are you going to do about it? Ever the bold nemesis, it will rationalize the torture of millions of animal lives in its expanding labs at the top of University Ave, as something to help humanity. And which part of our humanity will be killed by killing our animal kin and denying even talking about it. Nano-tech, bio-tech, growing genetically engineered fuel crops. Hello . . . there is a web of life out here . . . talk to your biology, conservation departments. We know so little. With all our money and scientists we couldn't put Strawberry Canyon together again. And is it to be UC's gift to the world, inventing a way to make it financially feasible to destroy "fallow" and wild lands the world over, so americans can keep driving SUVs using biofuels? This is not my idea of progress. Frankly it is tough to keep up with UC's uncaring "progress".

Is People's Park a distraction? Is it a real example of resistance? There have been few victories in stopping the UC steamroller. It's kind of a stand-off. What does the Park matter now, as the world changes on large economical and ecological scales? I think it holds some secrets we will need to make it through the changes. Secrets like Sharing, Diversity, and Loving the Land. It is an ecological arc and one of the most fertile and productive acres in the neighborhood. People's Park can show us how to turn asphalt to food gardens. And how to take care of each other.

As a bulb that pushes through the black dirt , we seek light, the truth, the promise of something new. Justice, Peace, Life, Freedom; can it bloom in the compost of chaos? Can we hold this land open and free enough to keep blooming? Can we hold away the jealousy, the fear, that want to control through concrete and pain?

Push, little bulb, push! We need your sweetness. Surprise us with your beauty. We need the Park.   —Terri Compost, 2009

....

Terri Compost came to People's Park before the construction of the Volleyball courts, for Mojo and Africa's free circle picnics in the late 1980's. She learned a lot by watching the University of California ignore the recommendations of Berkeley's Parks and Recreation and Landmarks Commissions and the pleas of so many residents. She saw the University force two big volleyball courts down our collective throats. She met a lot of her community and friends when we resisted. She has been to a lot of meetings about the Park. Terri began gardening in the Park's Community Garden after Rosebud Denovo was murdered. She really wanted to grow seeds and play in dirt as a way to heal. Lisa Stephens and experimentation taught her a lot. Terri has been gardening in People's Park most Sundays since. She teaches about organic gardening, foraging, native plants and urban wildlife. She has even taught about eating snails and acorns. Terri really likes parks. She thinks it is crucial for the survival of her species for us to wake up and respect and reconnect with the web of life, of which we are part and which sustains us. She says urban gardening is a good way to start.

PEOPLES PARK Time Line

June, 1967 - University of California, Berkeley (UC) gets $1.3 million to buy a block of houses and small apartments between Haste and Dwight for future university expansion.

Spring, 1968 - UC acquires all houses on the block, some from unwilling sellers through eminent domain proceedings. UC evicts all residents and tears down the entire block.

Early 1969 - The vacant lot sits empty and strewn with litter and mud. No UC construction efforts are evident and funds are unavailable to clean up after demolition.

April 18, 1969 - A notice in "The Berkeley Barb" underground paper written by Stew Albert and inspired by Michael Delacour calls for people to come to the vacant lot to build a park.

April 20, 1969 - Hundreds gather to clear and level the ground, lay grass, plant trees and flowers, and build a playground. Park construction continues day-to-day for the next 3 weeks with increasingly large and diverse numbers of people participating.

April 30, 1969 - UC officials begin meetings with park supporters and promise that no university construction at the property will begin without advance warning.

May 8, 1969 - UC Chancellor Roger Heyns meets with park supporters including Wendy Schlessinger and repeats promises that UC will not start construction without advance notice.

May 15, 1969 - Bloody Thursday - Without warning, hundreds of heavily armed police seized the park at 4:45am and erect a chain link fence around the park. Several thousand people march from a noon rally on the UC campus to a police line on Telegraph Avenue near the park. Police fire tear gas after rocks are thrown and a riot ensues which continues until early evening. Sheriff's deputies — dubbed Blue Meanies by demonstrators — fire shotguns at fleeing demonstrators. James Rector is mortally wounded and Allen Blanchard permanently blinded after being hit by shotgun blasts. 128 people are hospitalized after being beaten or shot by police. By evening, almost 800 police have imposed a 9 p.m. curfew and ban on public assembly.

May 16-19, 69 - Three battalions of National Guard troops occupy Berkeley on governor Ronald Reagan's order. Attempts at gatherings, protests and planting flowers at other area vacant lots are broken up by police and troops. Many people are arrested, beaten and gassed.

May 19, 1969 - James Rector dies of his wounds.

May 20, 1969 - A military helicopter sprays CS gas over UC Berkeley campus after troops trap a crowd by sealing off all escape routes. The gas, which causes blindness and vomiting, drifts throughout Berkeley.

May 22, 1969 - Troops seal off six blocks of downtown Berkeley and arrest 482 people caught within the cordon. Prisoners are subject to extreme abuse in County Jail. In a UC referendum on the park, 12,719 vote in favor of the park out of 14,969 voting.

May 30, 1969 - A peaceful five-mile long protest march of about 30,000 passes the park. There are no incidents. The fence stays up.

May 8, 1972 - The fence surrounding the park is finally torn down during a protest against the mining of Haiphong Harbor in North Vietnam.

Spring 1974 - David Axelrod and a group of undergrads at Cal start an organic gardening, student-initiated course and negotiate gardening on People's Park.

Fall 1974 - The group decides to focus on perennial natives arranged by CA plant communities and changes group name to People's Park Project/ Native Plant Forum, eventually affiliating with the Associated Students of the University of California (ASUC).

1976 - Osha Neumann & Brian Thiele paint People's History of Telegraph Avenue mural on Haste St.

1979 - People's Park Project/ Council builds the free speech stage for 10th anniversary

Fall 1979 - UC paves over the west end of the park which had been used as an informal free parking lot to make it a student fee parking lot.

Nov. 15, 1979 - The community vegetable garden on the west end of the park is created when people rip up pavement from the fee parking lot and use it to build landscaping berms.

June 14, 1980 - Riot ensues after police shut down a concert in the park.

Summer 1984 - UC police remove children's playground equipment that park supporters had installed in the east end of the park.

May 9, 1989 - Catholic Workers tow the People's Cafe, a retro-fitted house trailer, into the park in the middle of the night and start serving free food to homeless from the cafe. UC police remove it several months later.

1988 and 1989 - UC police repeatedly remove partially constructed restrooms that park supporters attempt to install at the park.

May 19, 1989 - A march to commemorate the 20th anniversary of James Rector's death turns into a riot on Telegraph Avenue.

Feb 6, 1991 - East Bay Food Not Bombs organizes to serve free lunch in People's Park. Serves five days a week continuing still in 2009.

July 31, 1991 - UC police seal off a portion of the park to build sand volleyball courts against the wishes of park users. Three days of street riots and police violence follows. Daily protests against the volleyball courts continue for months.

Dec. 15, 1991 - A park supporter uses a chainsaw to cut down the wooden central post of the volleyball court in broad daylight, and then escapes arrest.

Jan. 10, 1992 - UC files a lawsuit against key park activists to punish them for volleyball related protests and to intimidate would-be protesters

Aug. 25, 1992 -- Park activist Rosebud DeNovo is shot and killed by police after she breaks into UC chancellor's residence. Riots follow her killing.

Jan. 11, 1997 - UC removes its volleyball court in response to total non-use and constant protest. Park supporters roll sod over the ground the court once occupied.

Spring 2005 - Mural of the 1990's painted by Trish Tripp, Elvijo and friends, installed in old Berkeley Inn lot, across from 1976 mural on Haste and Telegraph.

April, 2005 - Free clothing exchange box is burned down by unknown arsonists.

Nov. 16, 2005 - UC police tear out a steel replacement free box built by park volunteers. UC police tore out other replacement boxes in Sept. and Oct. 2005 and have torn down any attempt to build a free box at the park since.

Thanks!   Dedicated to: The Future Warriors and Tenders of CommonLands and People's Parks.

Thanks to: Lydia Gans, Robert Eggplant, John Tanghe, Harold Adler, David Axelrod, Michael Delacour, Charles Gary, Mary David, Darla, Mac Nixon, Arthur Fonseca, Lisa Stephens, Ben Fulcher and Nadja, George Kalmar, Micheal Pachovas, Gina Sasso, Dusk, Dale the Gardener, Dana Merryday, Amy, Danny McMullan, Katy, Tommie and Nick, Kriss Worthington, Dona Spring, Gus Newport, Paul Sawyer, Maudelle Shirek, Carol Denney, Micheal Lee, BlueSky, Bruce, Eli Yates, Nancy Delaney, John Michael Jones, Gray Shaw, Molly, Stew Albert, County Joe McDonald, Utah Phillips, Hal Carlstad and Cynthia Johnson, John Benson, Shun, Dan Miller and Spiral Gardens, Stephanie May, Xarick, Janell Wheat, Marcus, Ashley and Kuma, Thu Ha, Sistar, Judith Gips, Jenny Yang, Andy, Gilbert, Tom the Artist, Bill, Tibor, Angela Rowen, Rev Jim, Soul, Peter Ralph, Joe Leisner, Charlie, Phoenix, Catherine, Christopher, Ron, Victor, Teddy, Chris Shein and WildHeart Gardens, Ocean, Yukon Hannibal, Turk, Orlando, Ray, Eddie Yuen, David Solnit, Phoenix and After Buffalo, Bill Lackey, Hadley, Bonnie Epslinger, Danielle, Marcus, Lisa, Boona, Kait, Sasha DeBrull, Daryl Dorris, Gary Seargent, Jake, Jane Welford, Jeff Ott, John Light, Monk, Mika, Paul Bloom, Peter Forni, Ramin, Ray Reece, Red, Pogo, C. Beck, Al, Christopher McKinney, Osha Neumann, Robert Scheer, Trish, Elvi Jo, David Beauvais, David Linn, Clifford Fred, Jim Chanin, Dean Tuckerman, Jesse Palmer, David Modersbach, Matt Taylor, Pat Wright, Moby, Hateman, Caleb, Doug Minkler, Russel Bates, John Vance, Mike Orr, Marc Weinstein of Amoeba Records, Mario y Rosalinda de La Fiesta Restaurant, Cafe Med, Kirk Lumpkin, John Ridder, Jerry and Dandy of 510, Tim, Rachel and Lew, Nick F., Bruce Sandcrab, Patrick Archie (Student for the Park), Chuck McNally, Wendy Schlesinger, Wavy Gravy, Eddie Monroe, Stoney Burke, Tamo, Ella the Dog, Steven Rood, Abby Rood, Stewart, Pacheco, Michael Veniziano, Matt Dodt, Bilge, Zoe, Helen Finkelstein, Vince Johnson, Hali Hammer, Gatsby, Christopher Masey, Michael Diehl, Debbie Moore, Jon L., Crow, John Gruey, Alice B., Ayr, Alex, Frank Bardacke, Jon Read, Bob Nichols, Mario Savio, Fred and Pat Cody, Heidi Starr, Travis, Zappa, Jody, Tim, Nadine, Sage, Mokai, Clan Dyken, BamBam, Lucy, Chocolate, Donut, Ginger, Dominique & Melissa, Enola, Tree, Cityzen, Loraine, Dumpster, David Blackman, Steve Brady, Shan Mesuda, Andrea Prichett, Shelley Doty, Max Ventura, Al, Tristan, Becky O'Malley, Sim Van der Ryn, Nora, Lisa SF, Kerry Liz, Juan Carlos, Jason Meggs, George Franklin, Glenn Turner, Diamond Dave Whitaker, Dorrit G., Sheryl, Sylvia Bagge for sharing her beauty and hoola-hooping, Julia Vinograd the Bubble Lady Poetess, Sam Davis (the good one), Andrea Moore, Sue Supriano, Emmanuel Sp., Sally Hindman, Father Bill O'Donnell, William, Reggie, Tom Condit, Marsha Feinland, John Delmos, Stephen Dunifer, Jim Robinson, Dave Weddingdress and Kayla, Derek, Steve Laughing Deer, David Glaubman, Curtis Grey, Aaron Handel, Bonnie Hughes, Richard List, Al Winslow, Mojo and Africa, Cinnamon, Stewart, Jon Reed, Gary Mason of Wolf/Mason Architects, Kat Steele, Bob Stern, Lyn Slanetz, James Muldavin, Esteban Muldavin, Mark Weinman of Regent Press, Poncho Jaramillo, Guillermo Prado, Malcolm Margolin, Elihu Botnick, Alan Copeland and Nikki Arai and all who created the photo exhibit and book "People's Park" (1969), Gino, Holi, Greg Jalbert, Io, Julia, Gianna Ranuzzi, Peter Bluhon, Ace Backwards, Katie Brewer, Mike Bishop, Lesley Emmington, Jeff Conant, Guy Colwell, Mike Foot, Frances Townes, Amanda, Fred, Minjeong, Monica, Kingman Lim, Nick Bertulis, Marcella, Melissa Lin, Christine, Dave, Grandma, Robbie, Lisa, Robert, Ron, Martin, Greg Getty, William Strauss, Cheyrl McGuire, Sharon Hudson, Priscilla Birge, Zachary Runningwolf, Bev-I, Ko, Flower, Mouse, Joseph D. Lowe, Christopher Kohler, Jose, Brenda Prager and her son Mitchell, Caitlin, Louis Morton, Arlene, Micha, Ed Holmes, Miguel Altieri, Ignacio Chapela, Charles Schwartz, Ted Chenowith, Don Mitchell, Janice Thomas, LA Woods, Stephanie Thomas, Karen Pickett, Nichola, Lawrence Scheckman, Aris, Melody Sage, Carol Schemmerling, Matt is Matter, Those in the system whose heart was with the Park: Renee, Joan, Carrie, Weldon Rucker, Horace Mitchell, Bob Marin, even Devin Woolridge and Irene Hegarty. All the Photographers known and unknown, (especially those who helped get photos to this book); John Jekabson, Harold Adler, Virginia Hotchkin, Zachary Ogen, David Blackman, Bill Haigwood, Shu Yamaguchi, Pierre La Plant, John Spicer, Merideth Grierson, Michael Kinney, Rosevelt Stephens, Jonathan Taylor, Xtn, Grace Christie and Jill Hutchby, Allan Alcorn, Elisa Smith and Stormy, Dean, Steffy, Austin Long-Scott, Jerry Takigawa, Herb Grossman, Lou de la Torre, Howard Erker, Lonnie Wilson, Bil Paul, Ryder McClure, Kenneth Green, Roy Williams, Dick Corten, Prentice Brooks, Keith Dennison, Venee Cal-Ferrer, Micha Dunstan, Jane Scheer, Oakland Museum of California archives, Bancroft Library, Berkeley Public Library and their great History Room and the BOSS Archives donated there. Oakland Public Library, Berkeley Architectural Heritage Association, Berkeley Historical Society, Creators and tenders of the www.peoplespark.org. Artists, Poets, Activists, Free Thinkers, Gardeners, Builders, Listeners, Event organizers, meeting attenders, All Musicians who ever played in the Park, sound people, anyone who has ever sang or danced in the Park, or dropped off manure, wood or compost, Freebox builders, Everyone who has lent their energy and care to the amazing community projects that have nourished People's Park: East Bay Food Not Bombs!, Berkeley Free Clinic, Free Radio Berkeley and Berkeley Liberation Radio, The Long Haul and the Infoshop, Copwatch, People's Park Community Garden, The Barrington Collective, Free Skool, Terry Messman and Street Spirit, RHA Bearfest organizers, CalCorps volunteers, Berkeley Project, The Oakland Permaculture Institute, Bay Area Seed Interchange Library, Ecology Center, Berkeley Daily Planet, KPFA, Larry Bensky, Kris Welch, Berkeley Barb, The Rallyer, Slingshot, Beebo Turman and the Berkeley Community Gardening Collaborative, JC and everyone with the Catholic Worker, Krishnas, Habitat for Humanity, Pagan Pride Festival, All Nation Singers, The Funky Nixons (People's Park House band), Hip Hop in the Park, Seen Productions, Tyrone Ingram, One Love Festival, Berkeley Worms, IndyMedia, Nabalom Bakery, Rebecca Riots, Ashby Community Garden, Cathaus, Cheeseboard Collective, Arizmendi Collective, Bay Area Alternative Press, The One True Church of the Great Green Frog, Explicit Players, Art and Revolution, Gilman Street Project, Chateau, Lothlorian and Barrington Coops, The Phoenix Coalition, The Phoenix Project for UC Democracy, Eric Drooker, Antioquia, Everyone who defended the Oak Grove Treesit, SF Mime Troupe, and All who have ever donated clothes or food, volunteered in the Park or just enjoyed it. All those who keep the peace and care for others in the Park and everyone who volunteers for the common good.

In memory of the Believers and for the Believers yet to come: David Nadel, Judy Foster, Jonathan Montigue, Gypsy, Rosebud Denovo, Bob Sparks, Thunder, Donna Spring, Claire Burch, B.N. Duncan. For James Rector and Alan Blanchard and all who took a hit for freedom.   http://www.peoplespark.org

EVERYBODY GETS A BLISTER

TODAY

—John Benson

—John Benson

—John Benson

— Roosey Stephens

—John Benson

LAND THAT IS EVERYONE'S

The unincorporated association of People's Park users claims the land upon the ancient principle that responsibility for the Earth belongs to those who take care of it. The idea is articulated in Common Law. English Common Law, dating from the middle ages, carried through to Colonial America, and still applies legally when no applicable legislation is available. Under common law, abandoned property belongs to its users.
— **"Disorientation Issue", *Slingshot*, Fall 1991**

To the extent that it's considered a free space in people's minds, I think that's almost the most important thing. It's one of the few places people think of as a free speech zone or as a free space.
—**Nick, People's Park Community Advisory Board meeting Nov. 5, 07, recorded by Robert Eggplant**

People's Park is a place where everybody is welcome and I find it interesting how the park is painted on a regular basis by the university and many people who really don't spend any time at the park as a place to be fearful, as a place full of violence and scary people and the reality is that I'm there with my kids, my three children, on a regular basis and they love the park and they feel comfortable there... and I feel safe there as a woman, I feel safe having my kids there and what I have seen, in fact, is that homeless people are very regularly in a sort of protective mode around families.
—**Maxine Ventura, PP CAB meeting Nov. 5, 07, recorded by Robert Eggplant**

This park is a reality we made in blood and fear and trembling and joy. People have died for this park, people have been blinded for this park, people have been beat up and jailed for this park.
—**Osha Neumann, at rally April, 2000**

The fact is, the very existence of People's Park just pisses certain people off and they just happen to have a lot of power. They can't handle the fact that there's a piece of land in this city that they don't control.
—**John Tanghe, *Daily Cal*, April 2000**

People's Park is one of the sanest things about Berkeley. It is a monument to citizen creativity and love for life. I have my son Chris to thank for bringing me to this green haven of political decency. When I needed Chris' company or counsel, I could often find him there, with Ester, his beautiful wolf dog. Upon occasion I would join him to help prepare a holiday meal for all comers. I loved that. Chris is overseas now, but I know he is proud of having left behind for People's Park, a bench with trellis, that he helped to design.
—**Joanna Macy, Nov. 2006**

This is Holy Ground for Berkeley types.
—**Grey haired former UC student to his son looking at the Mural and talking about the Park**

—John Benson

I like People's Park. It makes me feel like one of the people again.
—**Guy on the stage, Nov. 28, 2006**

"It is unusual, if not unique, that a park should serve such a variety of people and have so much going on just about all throughout the day," says Brad Picard, landscape architect with the City of Berkeley Parks, Recreation and Waterfront Department
—**Lydia Gans, "The Radical Dream of a Space for All the People", *Street Spirit*, July 2005**

It's a place for unfree people to get free and for free people to get freer. It's a class-free place: one might see punk-rockers, burn-outs, fresh college kids, the creative and the occasional rich. One can relax or get up-tight, meet new friends and old. It's a place where urban farmers can experiment. It's even a place to find others of like mind and form a rock band—or maybe even an 'underground mag' like People's Park Press."
—**W.R. Wolf, *People's Park Press*, April 1981**

—Elisa Smith

—*John Benson*

Native Peoples lived with this land for thousands of years. The Huichin Ohlone were here when the first Europeans arrived, bringing disease and cattle grazing to what is now Berkeley.
— *Illustration by Michael Harney from "The Ohlone Way" by Malcolm Margolin. Heyday Books.*

—Berkeley Public Library History Online

—Berkeley Public Library History Online
Deaf and Dumb Asylum, 1877
(several blocks Southeast from Park, now Clark Kerr Campus after being seized by the University)

University 1950's plan to develop almost all of Southside.

Suggested University Housing Development
A is a living center for Men (near Men's Gymnasium).
B is a living center for Graduates and Faculty.
C is a living center for Women (near Women's Gymnasium).

At the time I was a nice liberal professor...the chancellor appointed me head of this new committee called Housing and Environment... One of the first things that came to us was that Bud, Earl Cheit, who was the executive vice chancellor, the real power on campus, said you know we're going to tear down these blocks on Telegraph. And I said, "For what?" He said, "Oh, ah, we're going to build a new medical school." I did some research and found out there was nothing in the long term budget of the University for a medical school in Berkeley. So I said "No". And so we voted, they wanted us to basically okay this, and the committee said no, there's no justification for this, it's not in the long term budget or anything else. But they went ahead and cleared those blocks.
—Sim Van der Ryn, interview Nov. 8, 2007

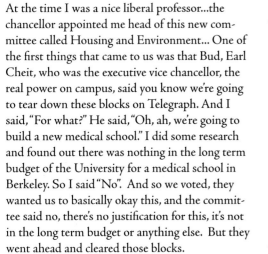

2541 Dwight Way

Through privileges of Eminent Domain the University of California bought a nice tax-free chunk of land in Berkeley, gave the over 200 residents living there notice to "quit and deliver up possession of the premises," and brought in steam-shovels which religiously gobbled up the emptied friendly old houses along with some bushes and a forgotten toy or two. Well-fed and clanking their chops the steam-shovels went home leaving the earth shorn and bleak. For almost a year it was left this way, absent of people and homes, prey to cars and ugly.
— Bonnie Fisher, "University can't allow the Harmony of the Park" *Daily Cal*, May 19, 1969

Illegal use of Eminent Domain by the University and low compensation to the landowners represents an abuse of state power; a seizing, a taking. Eminent Domain was abused in People's Park, it was political.
—Mark MacDonald, interview Sept 2, 2006

These were some of the 30 houses that were bought, through eminent domain if necessary, and demolished by the University in the block where People's Park is now.

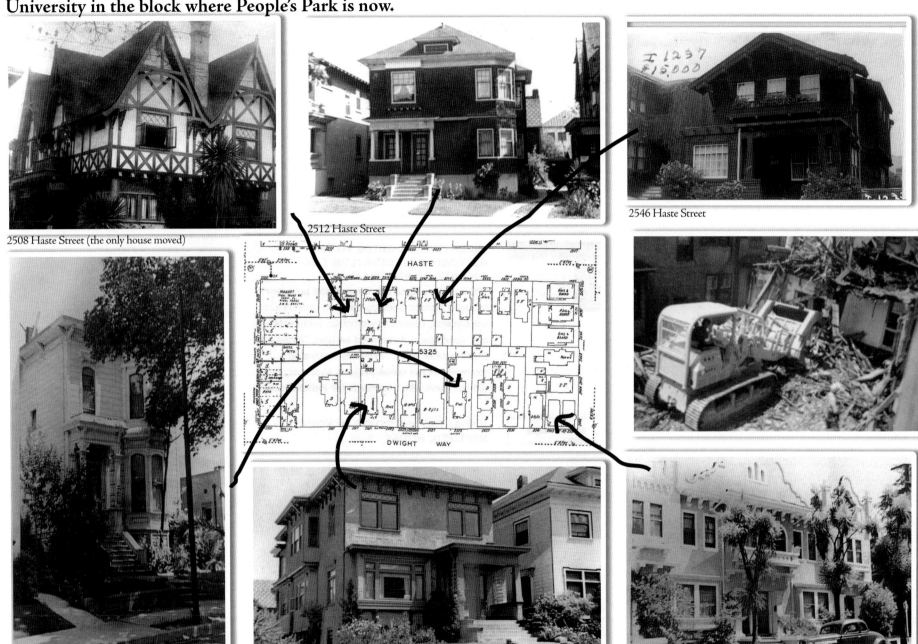

2508 Haste Street (the only house moved)

2512 Haste Street

2546 Haste Street

HASTE

5325

DWIGHT WAY

2529 Dwight Way

——*all house photos by Ormsby Donogh, tax assessor, courtesy Berkeley Architectural Heritage Association*

2521 Dwight Way

2545-2551 Dwight Way

—Daily Cal photo Tim Zukas

—Daily Cal photo Mike Lovas

Before and After--The picture on the left shows a row of houses on Haste Street slated to be torn down in the University's latest expansion. The buildings, most of them constructed before the turn of the century, have been converted into student apartments. Despite their age, the houses are well constructed, and have been tradition-ally popular with student residents. The lot on the right, formerly occupied by similar buildings, will soon be paved over for parking. Other lots will become recreation areas and eventual dormitories.

—**The Daily Cal, Feb. 15, 1968**

Many believe it was hostility to the hippies rather that the urgent need for playing fields which motivated the University's action.

—**David Lodge,** "People's Park and the Battle of Berkeley" *Write On, 1969*

"I want the University to tear these houses down to the ground and build parking lots, tennis courts, anything." Mulford (State Assemblyman) was furious that the University rented many of its dwell-ings to beats and runaways. He promised to get special funding to buy and demolish old houses. "We must get rid of the rat's nest that is acting as a magnet for the hippie set and the criminal ele-ment," he insisted. Mulford delivered the promised funds, and in July 1967 the University used $1.3 million to buy the remaining property that it did not own in the block above Telegraph between Haste and Dwight and prepared to demolish the entire block...It was December 1968 when the last building fell. Thus, for more than a year residents, former residents, and neighbors watched and reflected upon the transformation of a block of old but habitable dwellings into a vast urban wasteland.

—**W.J.Rorabaugh,** *Berkeley at War,* **1989**

My building was torn down. It was at 2523 Dwight Way... I lived there. I was enrolled at Cal full time and sometime around finals in the winter of 67...I got an eviction notice from the University of California. I was in the middle of final exams so I went down to Oxford Hall... on University Ave., that was where the administration was at that time. I went up and I said look,
I got this notice and they said, yes we're going to knock down the whole block. Everything which is where the Park is now was all houses. In fact, on Haste Street, on the northeast corner, where the palm tree is now, those were all beautiful brown shingle houses...They said yes, we're going to knock all the houses down and we're going to build a dorm there. I said, I'm in the middle of final exams, they said where do you live, and I told them and they said that they had done a study and that there were no students in my house. In fact at least half of the people in our house were Cal students. So I got very angry and I argued with them. Now I know I could have had it extended because it was a 3 day notice and they had to give a 30 day notice, but at the time I was a 20 year old kid and I really didn't know that...So I moved to another location in South Berkeley. After that, my house stood until about May of 68, I don't remember exactly. And then it was knocked down. Oh and they told me, once they found out I was a student, they told me when the dorm is built you'll be one of the first to get a place. That was almost 40 years ago. After the place was knocked down and the other places were knocked down they didn't build the dorm. It just stayed there. It was a big mud hole.

—**Jim Chanin,** interview, Nov. 2006

THE REGENTS OF THE UNIVERSITY OF CALIFORNIA

OFFICE OF THE TREASURER

OWSLEY B. HAMMOND
Treasurer

STANLEY J. THOMSON
Assistant Treasurer

2200 UNIVERSITY AVENUE
BERKELEY, CALIFORNIA 947

January 12, 1968

Mr. and Mrs. James Larick
2510 Haste Street
Berkeley, California

Dear Mr. and Mrs. Larick

    This is to advise you that demolition of the building in which you reside is scheduled for March, 1968. It will be possible, therefore, to continue your occupancy only until March 18, 1968.

    NOTICE IS HEREBY GIVEN that your tenancy from month to month at 2510 Haste Street, Berkeley, California, is terminated March 18, 1968, and you are hereby required to quit and deliver up possession of the premises to The Regents of the University of California on or before said date.

    This is intended as 30 days' notice to quit and deliver possession for the purpose of terminating said tenancy. You may terminate your tenancy at any time prior to said date by giving one week's written notice to this office. Any prepaid rent will be refunded to you. Rent due The Regents for a portion of a month should be paid in advance and may be calculated on the basis of 1/30th of the monthly rent for each day of occupancy.

    Upon vacating the premises, please deliver all keys to Room 615 University Hall, 2200 University Avenue, Berkeley.

    Arrangement for refund of any deposits held by us may be made upon return of the keys.

Very truly yours,

Eviction Notice from the Regents, Jan. 12, 1968

The University tore down my house (2546 Haste) last June and threw me and my furniture into the street. The brown shingled house in which I had rented a flat was just one of the 30 beautiful homes that lined Haste, Bowditch and Dwight and provided cheap housing for over 100 students. I had lived in my flat for over two years, and didn't really want to move. Nor did my landlord want to sell the property...he explained to me how he used the rents to pay medical expenses for his old and ailing mother, and how the university was giving him a lousy financial deal. But you can't fight them, he told me, because they have a long history of stepping on the little man as they expand without regard to those whom they hurt...What particularly irked me was the way in which the announcement was first made — the timing and words were used to make it sound as if the University was tearing down the houses in order to get rid of all the disruptive hippies that lived in back of the notorious "2400 block" of Telegraph Ave. Now first of all, I was not a hippy—I was a Teaching Assistant in Philosophy; and nearly everyone else who lived on the block (from Prof. Charles Sellers to the architect who lived next door) were connected with the University in some way. Secondly, even if the only people living on the block were hippies, what right did the University have to be going around tearing up THEIR homes?

—Michael P. Learner, 1969

—Dick Corten

Every Berkeley citizen suffers when the University tears down homes, because the city loses taxable property (the University gets its property tax-free) and so the property taxes on everyone else goes up.

—OutCry, 1969

Fighting a losing battle against what one student called "the University's severe case of manifest destiny" are landlords and student tenants of the area.

—Daily Cal, Feb. 15, 1968

—Mark Harris

The drone of University talk died and the people waited. The razed lot sat vacant. It was an eyesore compared to its previous elegant brown shingle houses; concrete foundations protruded through the sterile ground, staring out at the passing world with mudhole eyes. Garbage, broken glass and abandoned cars adorned the lot.

**—Allyson Kiplinger
"Case Study of Urban Ecology
and Open Space"**

Although ecological and environmental issues were raised by park developers and supporters, fundamental to the struggle was the right of ownership and the notion of private property rights. The park builders challenged the property rights of the Regents by declaring that the Regents had abused their rights and overstepped their authority by creating and maintaining a public nuisance.

**—Pat and Fred Cody,
"Experiment and Change in
Berkeley", 1978**

In the year before the May confrontation, there were four separate proposals for a community park on the land. The Chancellor's office ignored each one precisely because community use would have violated the very reason for the acquisition: to destroy rather than serve that community.

The idea for the park grew out of (Michael) Delacour's plan to hold a rock concert on the vacant lot in back of the Mediterranean. "I contacted this band called the Joy of Cooking to see if they'd play and they said 'Yeah'. So we went up and looked at the lot. The property was a mess— lots of broken glass, mud holes and abandoned cars. It was too ugly, so we called off the concert. We needed a park there."

—Robert Scheer, "Dialectics of Confrontation: Who Ripped off the Park" Ramparts, Fall 1969

The vacant land became an untended parking lot, full of pot holes, old beer cans, and weeds.

—Campus Ecologist, 1983

With the community houses leveled, a wasteland of muddy trash remained.

—Jessica Meyers, Sept. 12, 2006

—That Patch of Ground..Called People's Park, 1970

CREATION

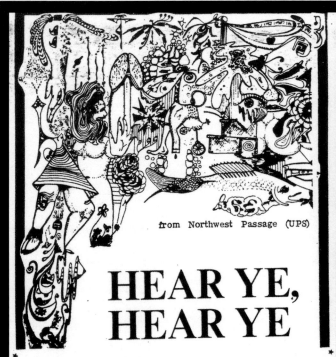

from Northwest Passage (UPS)

HEAR YE, HEAR YE

A park will be built this Sunday between Dwight and Haste. The land is owned by the University which tore down a lot of beautiful houses in order to build a swamp.

The land is now used as free parking space. In a year the University will build a cement type expensive parking lot which will fiercely compete with the other lots for the allegiance of Berkeley's Buicks.

On Sunday we will stop this shit. Bring shovels, hoses, chains, grass, paints, flowers, trees, bull dozers, top soil, colorful smiles, laughter and lots of sweat.

At one o'clock our rural reclamation project for Telegraph Ave. commences in the expectation of beauty.

We want the park to be a cultural, political, freak out and rap center for the Western world.

All artists should show up and make the park their magical possession. Many colored towers of imagination will rise above the Forum and into the future of reality. Pastel intertwining the trees and reflecting the sun, all Berkeley energy exploding on the disappearing swamp. The University has no right to create ugliness as a way of life. We will show up on Sunday and we will clear one third of the lot and do with it whatever our fantasy pleases. We could have a child care clinic or a crafts commune which would communicate its wares by having medieval-style fairs, a baseball diamond, a rock concert, or a place to think and sleep in the sun.

This summer we will not be fucked over by the pigs "move-on" fascism, we will police our own park and not allow its occupation by imperial power.

Come to the Dwight and Haste mud flat at one o'clock on Sunday, prepared to work and bring your own food picnic. When we are exhausted we knock off for rock music from "Joy of Cooking" and whatever bands show up.

"Nobody supervises and the trip belongs to whoever dreams.
Signed,
Robin Hood's Park Commissioner"

The Call to make the Park
—Printed in the Berkeley Barb Newspaper   April 16, 1969

—John Jekabson

Everybody was just desperate for some positive thing to do; something that could actually in a positive way give some public evidence, some polity evidence, to all the love and wonder that was brooding inside. We just wanted so much to make an affirmative gesture that wasn't an empty clenched fist against the oppressor, but actually planted something in the ground that could grow and could bare forth into the world, the kinds of health that we felt gathering inside ourselves intertwined with all the craziness and death of American society at that point.
**—Michael Rossman,
Claire Burch video interview,
People's Park Then and Now, 2008**

—*San Francisco Express Times* 5/14/69

For the first time in my life I enjoyed working. I think lots of people had that experience. Ever since I was eighteen I hated every job and either quit or was fired. But this was something different, with aching back and sweat on my brow, there was no boss. What we were creating was our own desires, so we worked like madmen and loved it.

—Stew Albert,
Berkeley Barb, April 25-May 1, 1969

The dreamers came out that Sunday afternoon ten years ago. Many came out of curiosity. Some out of a cynical desire to see another high-blown Berkeley experiment flame out... the last thing we expected to see...we saw. A bloomin' miracle!"

— "Rejoice People's Park is Alive",
Berkeley Architectural Heritage Association

The Park, in fact, appealed equally to at least three different sections of the community: its pastoral, pleasure-giving properties appealed to the hippies, its democratic and cooperative character appealed to the New Left, and its simple amenities appealed to many (though not all) of the local residents, especially mothers and children. An almost unprecedented community spirit emerged as people of all classes and walks of life worked together on the Park and used it.

—David Lodge, *Write On: The People's Park and the Battle of Berkeley*, 1969

Sunday in People's Park.

"Watch the pick."

"Want some lemonade?"

The island of sod planted last Sunday grows towards Haste behind the rakes and shovels of a hundred people.

"Everybody gets a blister."

Over in the corner, a group is building a stage, a stage with stairs and levels and a totem pole and a flagpole.

A father leads his daughter to the swing set that has appeared since last weekend. A mother sits on a table nursing her child.

Over by a deserted foundation another group is building a miniature Mexican garden with a grassy plaza and shaded walkways among the geraniums and sweetpeas. Just beyond the flower beds, beans and tomatoes are planted in the hard, sunbaked clay made soft by pick, shovel, water and loving care.

On the sod island someone has carved heavy timbers into a bench that seems to have been growing there for years. On the western edge of the park a cat is welding some steel tube into something.

You stand up to look around and, damn it, it is a park—at least, it's becoming a park, taking its form from the labors of nearly one thousand people.

—Steve Haines,
"A new kind of rest, work in People's Park"

A muddy, rutted piece of land stood vacant in the center of our community for over a year. For over a year, we listened while University committees, community groups, and others proposed the building of a park. We heard the University protest that it had no funds, that studies would have to be made, committees formed. Finally, we took the land. We tended it, loved it, planted trees, grass, and flowers on it, made it into People's Park... We were told we hadn't filled out the right forms, hadn't followed the correct procedures, hadn't been responsible, hadn't been patient. We had asked the wrong questions, and built a beautiful park. It was an incredibly good feeling, building that Park. In this country of cement and steel cities, better suited for its machines than for people, we made a place for people. At a time when only experts and committees qualified and certified, are permitted to do things, we did something ourselves, and did it well....Let a thousand parks bloom.

—c, "People's Park" 1969

—*Elihu Blotnick, Ramparts Aug 1969*

—*John Jekabson*

It caught on because it was a very special experience for Americans…It was a time when you were working and you were actually believing in what you were doing. People were building this park which they themselves were gonna use. There's no boss, right? They weren't working around their home but on the other hand they weren't working for money. They weren't like going here and laboring and not giving a shit about what they are laboring over, just get some money to go buy something else, it wasn't like that at all. They were building a park, they were making decisions about what should go in the park and there was no boss, and they loved it. It was like a completely new experience, for young people and old people alike. And it was a very, very joyous thing. And people came and they built the park and you can't really describe it to anybody who didn't see it. It was just beautiful.

—Frank Bardacke, "People's Park: The Big Four State Their Cases" Charles Palmer (former president, Associated Students, UCB), Frank Bardacke (People's Park Negotiating Committee), Wallace Johnson (Mayor of Berkeley), and Roger Heyns (Chancellor, UCB) Pacifica Radio Archives/KPFA, May 26 1969

Like who knows how many thousand others, I got involved in the battle of People's Park when somebody handed me a shovel and said, "Over there, we're breaking it up so we can lay sod down." Packed by weight of years of houses and months of cars, the hard earth barely yielded to any tool, had an oily blue sheen in the sunlight where it was cut. This was Sunday, April 20, behind Telegraph Avenue in Berkeley….I worked steadily for 20 minutes, then wandered through the diligent crowd. "Now I see how the Chinese build dams." No idle tools, and some dude in a cowboy hat was grading the bumps and hollows on a rented bulldozer. Wine bottles passed, lemonade, and joints from hand to hand. By dusk a rock band was playing and several hundred square yards of park had been laid down under old trees. In the next three weeks I came back time after time, bringing trees, poems and most of the children on my block…

— John Simon, "People's Park: Just the Beginning" *Liberation Magazine*, July, 1969

—Elihu Blothnick, Ramparts Aug 1969

We knew quite well it was university land and we didn't ask permission but we didn't set out to cause a fight. We set out to build a park…We didn't feel like we had to negotiate with anybody, it was not being used for anything.

—Frank Bardacke, interview Nov. 30, 2006

The People's Park is soulful socialism, the quality never experienced on the four-hundredth page of a dry textbook. We know what it is like to work without a boss to make the soil fertile with our dreams…The free men have a nation. It can be found slightly east of Telegraph Ave—we are very proud and patriotic and will not permit the beast bulldozer to cross our borders.

—Stew Albert, "Getting Serious" *Berkeley Barb*, May 2-8, 1969

—John Jekabson

—John Jekabson

—John Jekabson photos April 1969

—Allan Alcorn

—From "People's Park Berkeley CA 50cents" blue booklet c. 1969

—*Allan Alcorn 1969*

For the first time, hundreds of young people felt the sense of performing meaningful work towards creating a place of their own. Many students told me that the park represented their first real involvement in learning at Berkeley, a sense of participating in something significant and important. Many felt the joy of creating beauty in a city increasingly dedicated to ticky-tacky and asphalt. To me, much of the beauty and importance of People's Park had to do with the open process of planning and building. Anyone could take part in the concrete action of spontaneous design. Anyone could walk up to the park and plant a plant, and in so doing provide a genuine mooring place for his identity. Personal action produces a personal commitment.
—Sim Van der Ryn, "Building a Peoples Park"

A black teenager shinnies up a telephone pole and fastens on it a three part wooden plaque of his own making: "The People's Park." The name sticks.   **—Wendy Schlesinger,** ***The Whole World is Watching,* 2001**

With good will, with united effort, merchants, residents, architects, ministers, long hairs, short hairs, young, old, black, white, brown, yellow hard working enthusiastic Berkeleyans are together building something they all need.
—Grace Dilley, letter *Gazette,* May 16, 1969

—*Allan Alcorn 1969*

We were seeing ourselves as basically fighting for the children. The children loved this park. This was an unbelievably beautiful place and the energy, the multi-level, the strata, rich, poor, middle class, working, homeless, it was a place for everyone and it was incredibly compelling to be there, that energy was so full of love and joy.
—Anne Weills, 40th Anniversary Founders Forum, April 24, 2009

The park was born April 20, and it lived three and a half weeks. It is difficult to go back to the spirit of those days, when at first even the police were reasonably friendly. Decisions were made by the people who wanted to work, to lay sod here and plant a revolutionary corn garden there. There was a play area with several swings and a sandbox, but the favorite children's thing was a set of 7-foot high wooden letters spelling K N O W which could be crawled through. A platform festooned with prayer flags, brick walls, a maypole, a fire pit surrounded at night by the young passive drifters, far gone and not coming home.
—John Simon, "People's Park: Just the Beginning", 1969

—*Allan Alcorn 1969*

—*John Jekabson April 1969*

13

—*John Jekabson April 1969*

The places of refuge have vanished before the sprawling cities. Now new spaces must be carved out of our urban environment—spaces which are different from those around them which are distinguished only by a boring homogeneity.

— Gustav H. Schultz "People's Park: The Rise and Fall (?) of a Religious Symbol", University Lutheran Chapel

The felt need for a commons, a communal space, out ran the organizers' dizziest expectations...People's Park in the Northern California spring touched some deep hunger for a common life. It consolidated the community, made it palpable. It was an answer (however fugitive) to the question, "what do you people want?".

—Todd Gitlin, "The Sixties, Years of Hope, Days of Rage", 1987

Wendy Schlesinger 1969   —*Lou de la Torre*

—*John Jekabson April 1969*

—*John Jekabson April 1969*

But we find it impossible to deny that the park is at the very center of our struggle. The revolution is about the opening of time and space for human beings, inevitably the total liberation of the ecology. "The most revolutionary consciousness," says Gary Snyder, "is to be found among the most oppressed classes—animals, trees, grass, air, water, earth." The park has brought the concept of the Whole Earth, the Mother Earth, into the vocabulary of revolutionary politics. The park has raised sharply the question of property and use; it has demonstrated the absurdity of a system that puts land title above human life; and it has given the dispossessed children of the tract homes and the cities a feeling of involvement with the planet, an involvement proved through our sweat and our blood.

—John Simon
"People's Park: Just the Beginning"
Liberation Magazine, **July 1969**

Let a thousand parks bloom...

Calling themselves "agrarian reformers", the radicals announced that they wanted to establish on the site the model of a new cooperative society built from the ground up; that included growing their own "uncontaminated" food. One of the inspirations for the commission's act of civil disobedience was the example of the Diggers in seventeenth-century England, who had also seized public land with the aim of growing food to give away to the poor. In People's Park that food would be organic, a word that at the time brimmed with meanings that went far beyond any particular agricultural method.

—Michael Pollan,
Omnivore's Dilemma, **2006**

1976 Mural on Haste St.

I am referring to the so-called "People's Park" being developed on University property which may, on the surface, appear to be a most inocuous (sic) situation. It is anything but a harmless frolic. Located in the heart of the south campus crime belt this cleared land, awaiting development by the University, is being rapidly built into a hippie Disneyland.

...I have been informed by intelligence sources that this is not the spontaneous concept of Berkeley's "street people", but was conceived and is being directed by a clandestine revolutionary group specifically to precipitate a major confrontation with the police and the University administration.

—John K. DeBonis, Berkeley City Council
Member, Letter to DeWitt Higgs,
Chairman UC Board of Regents May 7, 1969

It should be obvious to every Californian that there are those in our midst who are bent on destroying our society and our democracy and they will go to any ends to achieve their purpose—whether it be a so-called park or a college curriculum.

—Ronald Reagan,
Sacramento Bee,
May 21, 1969

The park was "an engineered, contrived, phony, dishonest, agit-prop event", a plot by "the same tired old 'revolutionary' groups" and individuals.

—Mike Culbert,
executive editor of the *Gazette*

The place grew as weeks went by, hundreds of us turned into many thousands, people of all ages and races working together to create something. People planted trees, hoed gardens, brought in sod, made paths, cooked meals and fed everybody, made music — in other words, we defied the media image that we only hated and were lazy and destructive. I learned, for the first time, what democracy really meant. All decisions on what to build—be it a childcare area or a stage or a swimming pool—were reached by consensus of all participants. I understood clearly what taking control of one's life and environment meant. Ronnie (Reagan) couldn't hack the idea catching on. So, he sent in every police force in the Bay Area and the National Guard.

**—Tim Yohannan,
"Threat by Example", 1991**

When the Park-makers talk about the Park, they glow: when they talk about the fence, they become grave. The Park is physically, touchable, verifiably there, not just for its makers but for any eyes and hands. "Serving the people" requires physical proof, and the Park was that. Straight people were welcome, and they used the Park...Public need and vision collided with property. The friction between irrepressible need and immovable institutions ignited a war...As substance and sign of a possible participatory order, as the living and hand-made proof that necessary institutions need not be overplanned, absentee-owned, hierarchical—as such the Park came to stand in many minds as one tantalizing trace of a good society, as the practical negation of American death, as a redemption worth fighting for. Suddenly, almost inescapably, citizens were asked to choose between the splendid, self-ordered reality of People's Park and images of Chancellor Roger Heyns with his committees and charts and literally murderous lies.

**—John Oliver Simon,
"The Meaning of People's Park"**

Even today, when people ask me, 'What would your personal view of heaven be like?' I say, People's Park. It was incredible. People were growing vegetables. There were people building swings, building play structures. There were people trying to dig out a pond, people laying sod, planting rose bushes...There was a real kind of Walt Whitman on a Sunday afternoon thing: a kind of blending of play and work." **—Stew Albert,
1989**

The spirit that went into the park...was magnificent. It was also a frightening condemnation of the society...For what is being sought is an extension of participatory democracy to a degree of which we have had, until now, only the faintest glimmer.

**—Fred Cody,
"Cody's Books", 1992**

—Allan Alcorn

—John Jekabson photos April 1969

—John Jekabson photos April 1969

—Photos John Jekabson

Did no one see the harmony of hands and feet and backs and souls that turned it from a puddle-riddled mud glop, into an invitation to taste of sunshine, to feel grass in your toes, to swing in the sky, to eat around a fire, to know the stranger—human being you share the air with and the cold sidewalks—the harmony that was its pulse?
— **Bonnie Fisher, "University Can't Allow the Harmony of the Park"** *Daily Cal*, **May 19, 1969**

Most of the initial inspiration for the park came from people who had become political through previous experiences with the system. But they represent that nonsectarian breed that has managed to get through Berkeley's ideological warfare with a sense of humor and spontaneity in tactics. They are the free spirits, the anarchists of temperament who are not only incapable of conspiring or even really planning as a group, but who also have a profound contempt for manipulation and a distrust of those who practice it...The people who came to work were the type that resists "leaders" and much credit is given to Delacour for having developed

a style of leadership that stressed example, rather than exhortation. He simply worked the hardest at different jobs. If the leadership had been more heavy-handed it would undoubtedly have failed. As it was, it served to pull people together and work became a joyous thing.
—**Robert Scheer, "Dialectics of Confrontation: Who Ripped off the Park"**, *Ramparts*, **Fall 1969**

They have to understand what that park meant to us. It was a place in that area that was an expression of a new kind of community feeling. There were no fights in the park, there were no assaults in the park, we policed ourselves, I think the second week there were complaints from some neighbors about the music was too loud at night and we got ourselves together and policed ourselves and there was no loud music in that park after 11 o'clock. That rule was never violated. We policed ourselves, we were together. I used to bring my son every morning, I have a 17 month old son, I used to bring him every morning to play on the slides there and there was always a few other people around, and every-

one would take care of him, and we would talk about the park and our plans for the park. It was a beautiful expression of community initiative about what people can create if they take initiative on their own...And it's being taken away from us by a few men, not by the University, by a few men, who are afraid of that kind of initiative, afraid that people are going to begin to make decisions for themselves, and express freedom and build for themselves and create for themselves.
—**Frank Bardacke, Pacifica Radio Archives KPFA, May 26,1969**

And then the meetings began—sometimes two and three a day—between University officials and the park committee, the Telegraph Avenue Concerns Committee, and other ad hoc groups. It all came to naught. The University representatives had no authority to do more than listen and try to put their views across.
—**Pat Cody, "Cody's Books", 1992**

—Kenneth Green, "Azalea", May 18, 1969 The Oakland Tribune Collection, the Oakland Museum of California. Gift of ANG Newspapers

—John Jekabson

—Harold Adler

—Harold Adler

On May 6, 1969, Chancellor Heyns held a meeting with members of the People's Park committee, student representatives, and faculty from the College of Environmental Design. He set a time limit of three weeks for this group to produce a plan for the park, and he reiterated his promise not to take action without prior warning.

—"People's Park", Wikipedia.org, Nov. 30, 2008

—Keith Dennison, "People's Park Protest", May 16, 1969, *The Oakland Tribune Collection, the Oakland Musuem of California. Gift of the ANG Newspapers Museum*

I got a call from the chancellor and he said "I'm leaving for Washington tomorrow and we can't do anything about it, the governor's ordered that this fence go up". I said "You're leaving for Washington? You're the chancellor!". He says, "No well yeah, but I'm just a "Janitor for the Regents". I remember that line. That moment was my conversion from an upwardly mobile liberal professor to really being radicalized. I realized how empty these institutions really are. And then he says, "But we're soul brothers". And I said, "I don't think so".

—Sim Van der Ryn, interview, Nov. 8, 2007

Thursday May 15th
At 6am the ominous zooming,
war-sound of helicopters
breaks into our sleep.
To the Park:
ringed with police.
Bulldozers have moved in.
Barely awake, the people-
those who had made for each
other
a green place-
begin to gather at the corners.
Their tears
fall on sidewalk cement.
The fence goes up.
Everyone knows (yet no one yet
believes it) what all shall know
this day, and the days
that follow: now, the clubs, the gas,
bayonets, bullets. The War
comes home to us...

—Denise Levertov, "Green Flag" City Lights Books 1969

—Harold Adler

—Virginia Hotchkin, courtesy James and Esteban Muldavin

—*Leigh Athearn, courtesy Glenn Turner*

Quaker Vigil   —*Virginia Hotchkin, courtesy James and Esteban Muldavin*

What to do? What to do? A couple of the braver lads climbed the tall pines in the center of the park; it'd be hours before they were discovered. We could see down Bowditch Street to the University; when they came, they'd come from there. More cop cars gunned past, and again and again the rumor flew: they're coming. And finally…It was quiet. I remember that silence. The streetlight fell on their bobbing helmets; they looked like blue bubbles bobbing down the street. Then you could hear their boots. In America we were hearing boots….CHP –California Highway Patrol. Reagan was leading off with his best troops. They moved in quickly, cutting off the corners, emptying the Park. We faded back to face them across the street, a no-man's-land of asphalt. "Please go home," one officer said. And one brave fool, awoken to self-evident truth on the morning of this bloody Thursday, replied, "This is my home."

—Guy Lillian, "People's Park"
Challenger #2, winter 1995

What now becomes clear is that a war has been declared upon our community. Behind the Orwellian rhetoric of "cleaning up the South Campus area," the University and civil authorities have decided to deal with the problem of political opposition by destroying it—in the manner of a Vietnam pacification effort…We must talk to them about the oppressive institutions that prevent people from cooperatively improving their environment, and we must demonstrate—by example—our alternatives to those institutions. **Power to the People.   Don't Fence Us In.**

— flier "Our Park and Our Struggle"

Berkeley policeman putting on mask next to the cut fence, —*Merideth Grieson*

—*photographer unknown*

Thursday, May 15—12 Noon-Rally and march scheduled to meet at Park cancelled. Rally announced for Sproul Hall Steps. Speakers at rally included author Paul Jacobs, the Reverend Richard York, poetess and faculty member Denise Levertov, Michael Learner, a UC grad student, and ASUC President-elect Dan Siegel.

—"A People's Park Chronology",
1967- May 30, 1969

"On May 6, 1969, Chancellor Heyns held a meeting. Roger Heyns and the University Administration got together and decided they had to come up with a cheap way to use that land so that they could justify pushing the people out. They had originally bought that land, you know, to put dormitories on it, but they do not have the funds to build dormitories. And they had been, until the people started building the park, content to let other people use it as a parking lot. The new scheme as you know, is to build a soccer field, a soccer field that is not wanted by students here, is not wanted by people in the community and is not needed on the South campus area. There is a big field between Channing and Haste and that field is usually empty. There are also fields to the side and behind the Hearst gymnasium, those fields are usually empty. There is another field on the other side of the men's gymnasium and that field is usually empty...Let it be clear who is causing the confrontation. Who wants to show that he is cruel. It is Roger Heyns. What people have to do is to get themselves together to decide for themselves that they are not going to allow their lives to be robbed by Roger Heyns and the rest of those bums who escaped down to UCLA Thursday and Friday so they wouldn't have to be here to face the People...

Now we have not yet decided exactly what we are going to do. I have a suggestion, Let's go down to People's Park (cheering)... If we are to win this thing it is because we are making it more costly to the University to put

—*Bill Haigwood*

up its fence than it is for them to take down their fence. What we have to do then is maximize the cost to them, minimize the cost to us, so what that means is, People be careful, don't let those pigs beat the shit out of you, don't let yourselves get arrested on felonies. Go down there and take the Park.

—Dan Siegel, May 15, 1969 noon Rally Sproul Plaza

Then fate took a hand. Just as he delivered the line about taking the park, university police yanked the power to the sound equipment, turning what had been just another line into a clarion call for action.

—Michelle Locke, Associated Press
"People's Park Gets New Life"
Orange County Register, April 19, 1999

—Bill Haigwood

—Jon Jacobson

—Jerry Takigawa

It was difficult to credit that all this had happened because of a park, a little park. You would have rubbed your eyes in incredulity, if you were not already rubbing them because of tear-gas irritation. Yet in the apparent triviality of the issue lay its significance, and the reasons why it plunged Berkeley into what was probably the most serious crisis either the town or the University has faced...Thus a familiar story unrolled of a well-meaning but weak-willed administration caught between two extreme and mutually antagonistic pressure-groups, trying hesitantly to find a compromise solution, and then being panicked into making the wrong decision at the wrong time...the whole episode of the People's Park seems like a grotesque parody, in microcosm, of the Vietnam War...The parallel was certainly not lost on the young people of Berkeley.

—David Lodge "The People's Park and the Battle of Berkeley", *Write On,* **1969**

Thursday morning, May 15, 300 police in battle gear surrounded the park at 4:45 a.m. and ordered us out. Hopelessly outnumbered, we stumbled through their lines to watch workmen putting up the fence. Exhausted, tears of rage, tears of grief. And then at noon 5000 people whooped down the Avenue from campus to do battle. Everybody knows about Bloody Thursday, the shotguns, the death of James Rector. The days became indeterminate ages of confrontation, continual fear, meetings to all hours; too close to it to be a historian, I can offer an incident or two to give a sense of how it was...Late afternoon, Bloody Thursday, quiet south campus street, woman with baby carriage, telephone repairman, street brother grazed earlier by pellets tells girl on lawn "they're shooting people on Telegraph." "Are you sure?" Then Blue Meanie (Alameda county sheriff) pokes his head around the corner and lets fly, wounding the brother again, missing the baby carriage and grazing the phone man who doesn't understand, "lemme go get his badge number" he cries and has to be held back gently, "no, he's not wearing a badge and if you go up there they'll shoot you again."
—John Oliver Simon, "The Meaning of People's Park"
Liberation Magazine **July, 1969**

On May 15, 1969—it was about 5:30 in the morning I was going to work...and then I saw them coming over the bridge, like literally hundreds of cops, a long line of highway patrol officers and I decided I wasn't going to work that day. I waited till they all passed, I made a U-turn and followed them up to see what would happen. I saw them starting to put the fence up, then I went to the rally at noon on May 15, then I went down Telegraph... and I got as far as Cody's and I got hit in the head with a tear gas grenade. It blew up

right in my face. If I wasn't knocked out it was pretty close. I fell down. The free clinic just started recently and they came and gave me some stuff, so I was OK...
Then I saw a police car get blown up

—Harold Adler

on Dwight and Telegraph, and then I saw them take out guns, and I ran and that's when they shot James Rector I'm almost sure...and then the cops came around a corner and I started running with this other guy and I got shot in the back. But I was lucky. We later learned there was this big van that came up with all sorts of bullets and they just reached in and grabbed whatever they wanted and started firing. So I got shot with rock salt or low grade bird shot #9... It left this big red welt on my back. I had this heavy leather jacket on so that was very lucky for me. But the guy next to me was shot with something else, because he started bleeding. And James Rector was shot with 00 buckshot which is really large, big, big shots. I didn't fall down, it hurt, but I didn't fall down. The other guy fell down, he was running right next to me. And then they went on campus and literally shot up the campus. They ran through the campus firing and eventually the demonstration broke up and that night they called in the national guard.**—Jim Chanin, interview, Sept. 29, 2006**

Early the second week of May, Chancellor Heyns of the University assured people there would be no midnight raids on the Park while negotiations continued...Yet on May 14, he approved plans for the 8-foot cyclone fence to be erected around the Park, empowered Sheriff Madigan to use whatever force he considered necessary to protect the Regent's land title, put Vice-Chancellor Cheit in charge, and, then, left town. The rest is history.
—Armed Profits Affinity Group, July 29, 1969

You can talk about reason but you have to deal with the actions of the University Administration and you have to match up the two and see how reasonable the University of California has been. What I want to know from Chancellor Heyns, is why he told the University Community there would be no action on the People's Park without 24 hour notice, why Vice Chancellor Earl Cheit told the University Community that there would be no action on the People's Park for some time, and then the Chancellor ordered, at 4 o'clock in the morning for a fence to be put up and left town, left town. He and Vice Chancellor Cheit left town and left control of the situation in the hands of Sheriff Madegan who gunned down people in the streets.

—Frank Bardake, KPFA May 26, 1969

Jim Chanin, now an Oakland lawyer, was near the theater when the shooting started. "I saw people who were bleeding. It was like you'd see in some sort of totalitarian country," he says. "It was like, here I was brought up in the '50s—Mom, Dad, apple pie—and I'm seeing something that is completely at odds with that. It was only later that I became really angry."
—Michelle Locke, AP
The Orange County Register **April 19, 1999**

All I can say is that this is a beautiful sight. If these radicals want to fight with powder puffs fight them with powder puffs, if they want to fight with clubs, fight um with clubs, if they want to fight with guns, fight them with guns; they've got to be curtailed, this is a radical and a international conspiracy, this is a revolution but they're not going to win it.
—Berkeley Councilman Debonis, recorded in Berkeley, May 15, 1969

"The stream of water (from the fire hydrant) was directed at our forces and most of us got very wet. About this time missiles started flying from the crowd and a continuous barrage of rocks, bottles, bricks and short lengths of water pipe, and 12 to 18 inches long lengths of reinforcing rod started.

—Officer Hoeppner, "Haste and Telegraph Police Report" Bureau of Identification and Investigation

—from 1976 Haste St. Mural

There are grenade launchers being driven down Bancroft Way. There are bullet holes in your library, buckshot and bayonets in your students. The ammunition is up to 40 millimeters—we have a shell in our office if you would like to see it. And our anger increases with each day that you think shotguns will win you that park...If there was any question before, there is none now. The People's Park is ours. The people have earned it, and you have lost all claim on it. If you will not give it up, you still cannot have it.
— **"Do Not Provoke Thy Children"** *Daily Cal* **Editorial May 19, 1969**

The National Guard had simply closed off a large area of downtown Berkeley, arresting (480) shoppers and protester alike. I had a valid press pass...but Sergeant #1 would not let me leave the ring...Like others, I expected to be bailed out after a few hours booking at Santa Rita and then be home for a late dinner. Like the others, I was to be in a state of literal terror for the next 16 hours..."We have a bunch of young deputies back from Viet-Nam who tend to treat prisoners like Viet Cong" -Alameda Sheriff Madigan
—**Robert Scheer, "A Night at Santa Rita",** ***Ramparts,* Aug. 1969**

It is noon under the avalanche
of history, you are hanging between alternatives,
there are tears on your hands and earth
in your eyes.
—**Michael Rossman,** **Poem for a Victory Rally in a Berkeley Park** **for F.J. Bardacke   24 May - 15 June 1969**

Grace Christie and Jill Hutchby were working in their shop at Dwight and Telegraph, Berkeley Stamp Co. & Collectibles, ..."We saw terrible things that day," Christie recalled, "and the worst violence came from the 'Blue Meanies'"—deputies of the Alameda County Sheriff's Department so nicknamed for the turquoise blue jump suits they wore when working crowd control.
...Hutchby and Christie turned their store into a first aid center, keeping a supply of wet cloths for people who stumbled in with eyes blistering from the gas..."When it was over, we took them out through the back so they could leave by the alley," Hutchby said. "And then one kid came in with shotgun pellet wounds in his legs. He begged us for help and he said 'They're arresting us at the hospital,'" Christie recalled. The two patched him up the best they could and escorted him out through the back. A merchant we knew went out during a calm period, and when he was walking back into his store, they shot him in the back with birdshot. He eventually moved out of Berkeley."
— **Richard Brenneman, "The Bloody Beginnings of People's Park"** ***Berkeley Daily Planet,* April 20, 2004**

The Park was a little island of peace and hope in a world made filthy and hopeless by war and injustice...A university is supposed to teach, among other things, the Humanities. Are you, brothers and sisters who teach, going to let this inhumane thing happen, in your name—our name—the name of the University of which we, the Faculty, are a part—without a squeak? Do we believe in humane values, in constructive, creative life, or don't we? Or does the average professor—as many of the kids believe, or at least suspect—consider Property as sacred, and people and their needs and aspirations as dispensable?
—**Denise Levertov,** **"Human Values and People's Park"** letter *Daily Cal* **May 16, 1969**

To People of Color on this campus. It is all too clear that those who take a park away are of the same family that brutalize our communities, terrorize our women, and destroy the

essence of Freedom itself. Join in this struggle, we must see that their foe is ours...Power to the People. Power to the People of Color. Power to the People of Justice.
—**Third World Liberation Front, Steering Committee   May 23, 1969**

—*Harold Adler*

—John Jekabson

—Bill Haigwood

—Harold Adler

—L.M. Chase

—Harold Adler

PIGS SHOOT TO KILL-- BYSTANDERS GUNNED DOWN

—Scott Allen

WANTED

for MURDER

Chronology of Events

The Reality

The Lie

PEOPLE'S PARK

OUTCRY!

SAVE PEOPLE'S PARK

FROM OCCUPIED BERKELEY

POWER TO THE PEOPLE

LOCAL LAW ENFORCEMENT OFFICERS SHOTGUNNED DOZENS OF BERKELEY CITIZENS

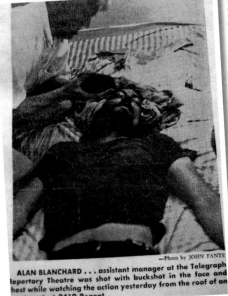

—Photo by JOHN FANTE

ALAN BLANCHARD . . . assistant manager at the Telegraph Repertory Theatre was shot with buckshot in the face and chest while watching the action yesterday from the roof of an apartment at 2410 Regent.

—John Fante, The Daily Californian, 5/16/69

By the end of the day, May 15, 1969, People's Park was fenced, dozens of people were in hospitals suffering gunshot wounds, a curfew had been imposed on the city and the governor of California, Ronald Reagan, had decreed a state of emergency and sent the National Guard to Berkeley. The city was under military occupation.
—People's Park: a documentary of "Bloody Thursday" in Berkeley

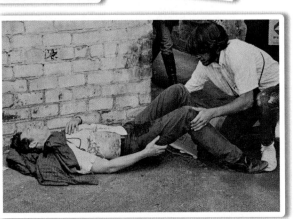

—Ryder McClure

A total of 53 persons, including five police officers and two newsmen, were injured in yesterday's riot. Twelve persons remained hospitalized today...At least 29 were treated for gunshot wounds. One was in critical condition, and three were listed in serious condition.
—Oakland Tribune, May 16, 1969

Riot Victim Dies
James Rector, a 25-year old student, shot during Thursday's riot died last night at Herrick Hospital.   **—The Daily Californian, May 20, 1969**

—Allen Alcorn

—Allen Alcorn

—Lonnie Wilson, "The National Guard Tries to Break up
Protestor's gathered at Sproul Plaza", May 19, 1969"
The Oakland Tribune Collection,
the Oakland Museum of California. Gift of ANG Newspapers

—John Jekabson

—John Jekabson

As you read this, Berkeley California is an occupied city. It is no different from Berlin or Saigon, or the dozens of other occupied "foreign" cities that you read about in the daily press....There is a curfew each night from 10 PM to 6 AM. No public gathering, assembly or loitering is permitted. Close to 2000 National Guardsmen patrol the streets. Why? What could possibly cause such massive force to be deployed in an American city? Why did they come down so hard?

—OutCry, 1969

—Roy Williams "Telegraph Avenue, May 18, 1969", The Oakland Tribune Collection, the Oakland Museum of California. Gift of ANG Newspapers

Berkeley began to look like an occupied city, with Army jeeps and trucks clogging the streets, helicopters patrolling the skies, and "Yanqui go home" scrawled on the walls. Protest marches of up to 4,000, though illegal under emergency edict, became a daily occurrence.

—Time, May 30, 1969

17 May 1969

As you must know by now Berkeley is occupied. The Nat'l Guard is here, the Calif H'Way Patrol, the County police, the local police—all the agencies of law enforcement have been sent in to hold down matters in the People's Park confrontation. It's strange walking or biking or driving around in the midst of all this. The Guardsmen are babies, probably young men, a lot of them, who wanted to stay clear of Vietnam. They strike up conversations with other passing Berkeleyans their age & smile a lot. All the other enforcement people are odious & professional, aimed, it seems, at hurting people.

25 May 1969

The war here goes on. Reagan refuses to comply with the request of the City Council & pull the troops out... Everybody's nervous & frightened. The spraying of the campus area with gas...by helicopter, harming lots of profs and "innocent bystanders" has radicalized the better part of the community overnight. **—Al Young, letters to Ted Wilentz, Bancroft Library**

And they began to talk to their brothers in the National Guard...."Take off your masks! Take off your masks! You are men, not machines! You are not our enemies. You are our brothers. Take off your masks!"...There's film of it that I saw later on television. I pray to God it survives. It shows the first Guardsman reaching up to his face and, with infinite weariness, removing his helmet, and with infinite sadness, pulling the gasmask from his face. He is young, crewcut, blond. He is weeping. He puts the mask into its pouch on his belt, so slowly, and so tired, and then he replaces his helmet and he stands there, at his post, tears streaming down his handsome young face. An officer runs up, or maybe it's a cop, screaming at the guy to put his mask back on. But the Guardsman just stands there and looks at the man like he was speaking Martian....All down the picket line gasmasks start hitting the ground.

That night I wrote in my diary, "We're going to win this thing. Reagan will be reelected and [Sheriff] Madigan will still strut. But their time is limited in this life. What [we] saw today is forever. We're gonna win."

—Guy Lillian, Challenger #2 winter 1995

So the national guard came the next day and demonstrations went on during the week. They declared martial law, they imposed a curfew. On May 19 I got arrested, I was on the corner of College and Ashby. I was watching this demonstration. What they would do is, it was sort of a terror tactic, about 10 of them (Highway Patrol) would walk up to people in the crowd and you would get selected. They'd just drag you away. So it was my turn... They handcuffed me, then the officer said that if he were my father he'd kill me and they threw me in a paddy wagon and we drove all over the city and that was the same time that they were spraying the campus with tear gas from the helicopter, the same day, May 19. They took me to jail and they charged me with loitering in a time of martial law,

a statute which has since been declared unconstitutional... I was in jail, it was Malcom X's birthday and everyone was singing happy birthday to Malcom X and the cops were very angry and I got bailed out and then they dropped the charges.

—Jim Chanin, interview, Sept. 29, 2006

—John Jekabson

—Roy Williams "National Guard at Shattuck Ave., May 16, 1969 "The Oakland Tribune Collection, the Oakland Museum of California. Gift of ANG Newspapers

—Virginia Hotchkin, courtesy of James and Esteban Muldavin

—Bill Haigwood

—Grover Wickersham

—Virginia Hotchkin, courtesy James & Esteban Muldavin

(Address to a National Guardsman)
You could as easily have been my lover
As the man who held a bayonet between us.
On the street we met but could not meet
with armies and universities for armor.
If only as children we could have embraced
And left the guns and books to become part
of earth.

—Judy Busc, "Green Flag"
City Lights Books 1969

—Howard Erker "People's Park Protest, May 30, 1969,
The Oakland Tribune Collection, the Oakland
Museum of California. Gift of ANG Newspapers

This is Corporal Feliciano of the National Guard, one of 2000 men called up by California Governor Ronald Reagan to bring a halt to the Battle of People's Park. The Guardsmen were used to herd the students from one end of the campus to the other, advancing with their bayonets before them. They put up barricades, manned them, flew over the area in helicopters,

cleared the streets and assisted in making arrests. After six days of this, the Guardsmen began to tire of the game. They are young men—many of whom are in the Guard because the prospect of serving more than six months in uniform is so distasteful. Feliciano and his squad were detailed to clear Telegraph. His associates hassled one student after another and finally Feliciano had seen enough. He threw down his helmet and his rifle and said he'd do no more. He wasn't about to put any more people through all this bullshit. He was arrested himself and taken away. The battle continues, meanwhile, with no light visible at the end of the tunnel.

But Tuesday was, in some ways, the most frightening of all, at least in its implications. Three thousand pro-Park demonstrators held a memorial march for James Rector. At 2:00 in the afternoon of a clear, warm, bright Berkeley day, some 700 stragglers had been surrounded in a tight ring on Sproul Plaza by Guardsmen.

...From the second-floor balcony of the Student Union came a garbled bullhorn message from a campus cop. "Chemical agents are about to be dropped. I request that you leave the plaza."...With that, all the cops and deputies and Guardsmen put on their gas masks. Then came the whack and whine and whir of a hulking brown Sikorsky helicopter carrying a bellyful of National Guard tear gas. It came low over the treetops, no more than 200 feet, laying down a veil of white, powdery vapor for 500 yards before it got to Sproul Plaza. Brigadier General Bernard Narre the field commander at the scene and who called in the helicopter attack later said, "It was a Godsend that it was done at that time."

From three sides, the lawmen and Guardsmen pitched tear gas into the crowd of demonstrators, who ran in all directions, screaming and shouting, trying to escape the biting, nauseating fumes. But there was no way out. Guardsmen had encircled the immediate area, and prevented demonstrators from getting out with the threat of their bayonets...The light wind whipped the tear gas all over the campus and surrounding neighborhood. Students rushed out of classrooms and housewives out of their homes in a radius far from Sproul Plaza. A school picnic in Strawberry Canyon, some 40 or 50 kids enjoying the outdoors, turning to squawling, parlicky chaos. The gas even seeped into Cowell Hospital, upsetting operations there, rendering nurses useless as patients gasped for breath and cried out. Said the manager of the hospital: "I protest that this is not what tear gas is for."

— **"The Battle of People's Park",**
Rolling Stone Magazine, June 14, 1969

—*John Jekabson*

We all thought the gas masks were for "tear gas" canisters like previously. We never thought a helicopter would fly over and drop CS nerve gas! We were dealt with like North Vietnamese—well, no napalm, but shotguns. Many people did think Berkeley students were commie scum. However, I was a graduate student in biophysics starting my research in radiation induced cancer. Had wife and two kids. I was very altruistic.... I was blinded for several minutes and grappled my way several hundred yards east to Barrows Hall where I washed my eyes with water. Then I walked through campus to my car at LBL (Lawrence Berkeley Lab) where I worked while a graduate student at Donner Lab near Founders Rock on the northeast corner of campus. I vowed at that point to let my hair grow. I was radicalized.
—Pierre La Plant,
notes on photos 1969-1971

—*Bill Haigwood*

May 20, 1969 March   —Pierre La Plant

—Lonnie Wilson "Helicopter Tries to Breakup People's Park Protestors Gathered at Sproul Plaza May 20, 1969"
The Oakland Tribune Collection, the Oakland Museum of California. Gift of ANG Newspapers

On Tuesday, May 20, 1969, Berkeley, a city in the United States, a university town with many suburban dwellers as well as the faculty, staff and students of the university, was attacked from the air by toxic gas from a helicopter. It was the first city within the continental limits of the United States to be assaulted by a helicopter flown by a member of the National Guard and under the orders of an elected official, the sheriff of the county. The gas was sprayed into an area where seven hundred people were confined by the National Guard in close formation. These people, these American citizens, had no means of escape from the gas that is used in Viet Nam to flush suspected Viet Cong from tunnels and dug-outs and caves. This chemical weapon is not mild in its effects: it irritates the eyes, it can burn exposed areas of the skin, and it induces projectile vomiting and instant diarrhea.

...How could this happen? How could an American city be attacked from the air by an arm of its own government?
—Dr. Thomas Parkinson, *Protect the Earth*,
City Lights Books, 1970
Senior Professor of English at UCB

Even some guardsmen questioned the use of gas on people who were prevented from fleeing the gassed area. Some of the part-time soldiers, in fact, were plainly skeptical about their whole mission. One guard corporal standing duty in a long line of troops, who had been blocking the south side of the campus, suddenly threw down his helmet and dropped his gun. "I can't stand this any more," he shouted, "I've had enough." He was quickly hustled away by MP's.
—Peter Barnes, *Newsweek* June 2, 1969

—John Jekabson

—Lou de la Torre

Alameda County Sheriff Frank Madigan Wednesday disciplined 10 officers, including the commanding officer of Santa Rita prison farm, for "irregularities" in handling Berkeley demonstrators arrested during the "people's park" protest....Many of those arrested accused Santa Rita guards of brutality, beatings, unusual vocal harassments and forcing the male prisoners to lie face down on the ground for several hours.

—"Sheriff Reprimands 10 Officers in Park Arrest Violations", *LA Times* July 3, 1969

The University had to choose—property versus flesh. They chose wrong. Seventy people were shot and one man killed to keep them from picnicking on University land.

—Charles Horman, June 13, 1969 Commonweal

The People's Park episode in Berkeley led to sympathy strikes across the state; we at UCLA, after all, were part of the same university system as Cal. In early May, following a very moving speech by someone I knew as a history teaching assistant for Western Civilization, a large number of us marched to the Administration Building and "occupied" it. We sat in the hallways and refused to leave. We held small group discussions on tactics all night. We were given the names and phone numbers of a couple of lawyers and told to write them in pen someplace on our skin, in case of arrest. Rumors of police being sent circulated all night, but none came.

—Ken Klein, world.std.com

A group of University Professors have organized a bail fund to assist the release from jail of the many students and other members of the University community who have been or are being arrested during the present University occupation. The burden of being arrested and incarcerated is a heavy one which is falling in erratic ways upon students and others seeking administrative responsiveness to University needs. Many will too share this burden—at least financially—and the present bail fund is one way... Among the organizers and directors of the bail fund are Professors David Krech (Psychology), Thomas Parkinson (English), Elizabeth Scott (Statistics), Otto Smith (Electrical Engineering), Roger Stanier (Bacteriology and Immunology) and Jack Block (Psychology).

—Bureau of Identification and Investigation, mimeograph May 23, 1969, Bancroft Library

University Regent Fred Dutton, one of the pre-Reagan liberals on the board calls the Berkeley situation the "most fascistic" he has seen in this country including Chicago at the time of the Democratic Party convention. And Dutton, is no raving radical. Just a plain liberal. "Students," Dutton notes, "were planting flowers in the first place, and in the long run of history, I would have to say that flowers beat fences. And that young men beat old men every time."

— "The Battle of People's Park" *Rolling Stone Magazine*, June 14, 1969

The San Francisco architectural firm which said it wouldn't work on the "People's Park" site student residences unless a users-developed park were included has made good its threat and quit the project...A letter mailed by the firm Aug. 4 to university regents said, "The current direction of urban design in this country is not being considered in the development of the site... The concern of the public can no longer be disregarded on those projects which directly affect the environment of the city".

—*Oakland Tribune*, Aug. 10, 1969

Beyond the smoke and confusion of last week's tragic events in Berkeley are some broader questions. When youthful citizens can be wantonly gassed and beaten, all because of a small, unauthorized park, what has happened to America? What has happened to our sense of perspective, our tradition of tolerance, our view of armed force as a last—never a first—resort?

—Peter Barnes, "An Outcry: Thoughts on Being Tear Gassed", *Newsweek*, June 2, 1969

— Bill Haigwood

— Pierre La Plant

All Fences Down!

On Memorial Day, May 30, the Park Committee
Asks All to Rally in Berkeley
Together

We Will March to Peoples' Park!

James Rector is dead in Berkeley of a police bullet in his heart. A sadistic Alameda County Sheriff's deputy killed him as Rector, from a rooftop, watched the massive assault on hundreds of brothers, none of whom he had met in a park built on vacant land. He was shot by a single policeman, but Sheriff Madigan distributed the shotguns, fired the police guns which shot a hundred others on the bloody day of May 15th. It swung the clubs which have wounded, even crippled, dozens of others since that day, in methodical, as tactical, conscious and indiscriminate violence.

Berkeley has undergone ten days of siege by 2700 National Guardsmen and thousands of police. All political and constitutional rights have been suspended by Reagan's fiat. A reign of terror - with heavily armed police trespassing and breaking into homes and dormitories has hit the university community.

All this because the University of California expropriated Peoples Park from the Berkeley community.
Is this for a park? But there are great things at stake, as we have learned with our blood. Reagan's troops and the University's police are the same as the occupation troops in Vietnam and the ghetto. The military attacks on Berkeley have been indiscriminate because the University's "enemy" is an entire community. The Telegraph Avenue community, which has long been in the forefront of the national youth revolt, built a park, People's Park, on land the University said it owned because it had a piece of paper. Land in this society is owned not because of human need...

MARCH IN BERKELEY MEMORIAL DAY

DEMAND THAT THE FENCE BE TORN DOWN!

On Friday, May 30, Memorial Day, come to Berkeley to join the mass protest against the killing, shooting, beating and jailing of our brothers and sisters... Join the march to demand amnesty and the immediate end of injunctions and dragnet arrests.

IT IS OUR CONSTITUTIONAL RIGHT TO HAVE THIS MARCH.
WE INTEND TO BE PEACEFUL.

INSTANT NEWS SERVICE

TODAY

Monday, May 26, 1969

·MASS ACTION·

12:00 Rally in Sproul Plaza. Rally will move to business district to picket those stores not displaying "SOD BROTHER" signs.

2:00 Rally in Provo Park to support those being arraigned.

3:00 Continue building People's Park annex at Hearst and Grant.

·UNIVERSITY EMPLOYEES·

All Day Concerned Student Employees of the University's food services are urging a boycott of the dining commons because the University is supplying food to the occupying forces. They will be picketing today in protest.

·BOYCOTT·

All Day Berkeley Coalition will be distributing leaflets urging a boycott of downtown.

·REAGAN LAND·

1:00 Massive (10, 000?) march on Reagan. Leave 4th St. and Capitol Mall - go 6 blocks to Capitol. Buses will leave U.C. Davis from 11:00 on. Reagan is not invited and will not be allowed to speak.

·VIGIL·

7-8 pm Berkeley Friends will hold a peaceful vigil for the park every night at the corner of Bowditch and Dwight Way. Everyone welcome.

·PARENTS·

8:00 Mass meeting of parents at Washington School (McKinley and Bancroft) to evaluate Saturday's march, plan further action, and elect a new steering comm. Spon. by Parents for Community Peace.

The Day in Berkeley

A BIG PEACEFUL MARCH

San Francisco Chronicle

FINAL

SATURDAY, MAY 31, 1969   10 CENTS

No. 130

Flower Power

A Big 'Park' Parade --- Sunshine and Dancing

Flower Power

...itons End
...alk Across
... Ocean

Thousands Turn Out
--- Nobody Is Injured,
Only Two Arrested

Instead of blood on the streets this hot May day, the people of Berkeley rolled out sod and grass: instant lawn. Instead of peppergas sprayed from the back of a jeep, rock music crackled forth from the back of a slow-moving truck. In answer to their flak jackets, cops looked on embarrassed and fascinated at the painful beauty of street girls naked to the waist...The Fence – barbed wire, entwined with flowers. It was spontaneous and it was unexpected, this answer of the people of Berkeley, the creators of People's Park, to the brutality and the cynicism that had taken it from them. It astonished me then and it astonishes me now, that the answer our brethren gave to gas and terror was that most delicate of symbols: flowers. Instead of blood ... there was brotherhood. **—Guy Lillian, "People's Park" *Challenger* #2 winter 1995**

FRIDAY, May 30—20-30,000 persons from across the nation joined a long peaceful march from the Annex to the fence. Flowers placed in fence. Sod laid in street. Sheriff's Deputies stationed on rooftops throughout area equipped with shotguns, tear gas and rifles. Marchers returned for celebration at People's Park Annex.
—*A People's Park Chronology from 1967 to May 30, 1969*

—Allen Alcorn

The great march was a mixed bag of beauty, defeat, triumph and foolishness. Ronald Reagan was unable to scare us off the street. The handful of conspirators turned out to be 35,000. But somewhere in the front of the march people forgot what it was all about.
—Stew Albert, "What did We Forget" *Berkeley Barb*

We are not implying that the March should have been turned into an insurrection, only that it fell far short of the kind of confrontation which was needed. We should have surrounded the Fence (like the Pentagon and Chicago Hilton were confronted) angrily exposing to everyone that only raw outside military force stood between us and our park.
—Frank Bardacke and Tom Hayden, "Free Berkeley", *Berkeley Tribe*, **Aug. 22, 1969**

At one point in the planning, someone mentioned the idea of having flowers to pass around and spread here and there among marchers. A local shop owner known to students as "Mother Earth" offered to handle the purchase of 30,000 daisies if money could be found. Norman immediately picked up on this. He had two loyal Service Committee donors, elderly sisters, who he felt might put up the cash. As he relates, ... "I went down to my little old ladies in San Jose and they gave me $3,000 for the daisies".
—Stephen McNeil, *Berkeley Daily Planet* **Dec. 24, 2004**

The demonstration itself was strange. The strain the city had been under somehow relaxed during it. People were very emotional, very close to each other, always very close to tears or laughter.
—Pat Cody, "Cody's Books", 1992

—Pierre La Plant

—John Jekabson

THE WAY WE DID IT | THE DAY WE DID IT

—Pierre La Plant

—Allan Alcorn

RESISTANCE & HOPE

THE FENCE COMES DOWN

—Don, Berkeley Tribe Oct. 16, 1970

But the fence was still there, and it still bothered us. As much as we tried to re-press it and forget it, the fence kept com-ing back into our minds. It was a thorn. It mocked us, dared us. It was there and couldn't be ignored, like a boot on the neck...The fence was not invulnerable. The system is not invulnerable. On July 14 we caught the pigs off guard and slashed the fence to pieces. We knew we couldn't tear it down for good, not until we had broken the power of the men who had put it up. But we served notice that we intend to do just that.
—**Ike Clanton "What It Means",** *Berkeley Tribe, July 10-24, 1969*

Then, in May of 1972, almost three years to the day since the fence had been erected, the desire to tear down the fence and "liberate" the park was finally realized. On the evening of May 8th, President Richard M. Nixon announced that he had ordered the blockading of North Vietnam and mining of Haiphong Harbor and other ports...Demonstrators flocked to the playing field and, by 11:30 P.M., had succeeded in bringing down the fence.

On the next day, after finding that it had been propped-up, hundreds of protestors "lined the fence around People's Park and with scores of fingers grasping the mesh, pulled it to the ground".
— **Stanley Irwin Glick, Dissertation, SUNY at Stony Brook, May 1984**

The fence stood for another three years, but on May 8, 1972, a violent demonstration against President Nixon's mining of Haiphong Harbor in North Vietnam turned into a storming of the park. Protesters tore the fence down and pried up the asphalt courts built by the University, throwing the pieces into the street. The fence was never replaced, but the western third of the lot remained a free parking lot for several years.
— **Don Pitcher & Malcolm Margolin, "Berkeley Inside/Out", May 19, 1989**

"I helped tear the fence down and it was a glorious feel-ing to free this earth again. I felt that our ideas had been imprisoned with the land."
—*San Francisco Chroni-cle, May 15, 1972*

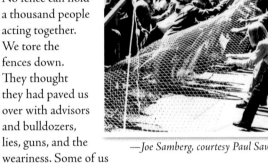

—Joe Samberg, courtesy Paul Sawyer

Our hands are a flower tearing up the asphalt that covered the People's Park. No fence can hold a thousand people acting together. We tore the fences down. They thought they had paved us over with advisors and bulldozers, lies, guns, and the weariness. Some of us thought so too. No one knew how to name the roots that kept growing.
—**Michael Rossman, "People's Park: Round Two", May 9, 1972**

One guy pushed on the fence and it created a wave mo-tion. We all began pushing with the wave. The standing wave got bigger and bigger and then boom the fence went down. Someone had a sledge hammer and began break-ing up the concrete and some started to throw pieces at a police car. Someone (maybe the city or something) sent in a back hoe and dump truck and tore up the concrete so we wouldn't have ammo. Then the dump truck, back hoe and police left. There were 400 of us left. Someone let out a rebel yell and a fire was lit and joints passed around. It was one of the best victories of my career, working in concert around that fence and bringing it out of the ground.
—**Llwyd Watson, Sept. 14, 2006, Save the Peaks Rally interview**

—*Pierra La Plant*

History of People's Gardens, 1974-79

The existing gardens of People's Park began in April 1974 as a student-initiated field study and evolved later that year into the People's Park Project/ Native Plant Forum, a student and community group affiliated with the ASUC. Our task was simply to revive the spirit and reality of People's Park, to use our best environmental tools and techniques to restore Mother Earth and thereafter, to keep hope alive...One of the first policies we adopted was to seek maximum consensus and cooperation among all parties and members of the larger community. Consistent with this policy, which has stood the test of time ever since, we approached the University of California administration. I set up a meeting with Bob Kerley, the U.C. Vice Chancellor at that time. We met, one-on-one, in an informal and cordial setting. Bob Kerley was a shrewd administrator, yet easy-going, amiable and collegial by nature. I sought only to inform the Vice Chancellor of our intentions, not to request permission. After advising and reassuring Mr. Kerley, he could see no problem with our pursuit of such a gardening project at People's Park, and accordingly, gave us the green light...That meeting would prove highly significant when the U.C. Police showed up that first gardening day...the officer took me seriously enough to get on his walkie-talkie and check it out. Anyone standing anywhere near the vicinity of the walkie-talkie quite clearly heard the voice on the other end crackle back, "Let them plant!"

Later in the summer of 1974, a fateful decision was made to evolve the nature of the Project from annual and temporary to perennial and permanent plantings. From the initial emphasis on flowers and veggies, we made a subtle but profound transition to woody plants, shrubs and trees, featuring California native plant species...We arranged the California native specimen plantings according to the native plant communities or ecosystems to which the particular species belong and associate in nature.

The rest, as they say, is history. Repetitive acts of gardening were committed on a daily basis. The tradition of having one major public planting day per week was adopted, eventually centering on Sunday.

—recalled by David Axelrod, Mar 3, 2009

—David Axelrod

—David Axelrod

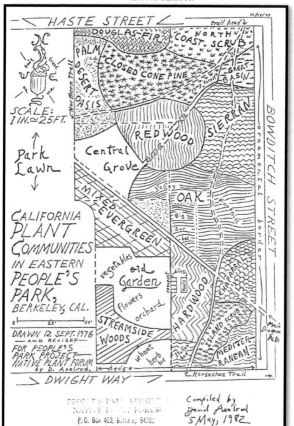

CALIFORNIA PLANT COMMUNITIES IN EASTERN PEOPLE'S PARK, BERKELEY, CAL.

DRAWN 12 SEPT. 1976 — AND REVISED — FOR PEOPLE'S PARK PROJECT NATIVE PLANT FORUM by D. Axelrod.

PEOPLE'S PARK PROJECT NATIVE PLANT FORUM P.O. Box 463, Berkeley, 94701

Compiled by David Axelrod 5 May, 1982

—David Axelrod

—Tjet M. Sun

The west end of the Park was used as an open "People's Parking Lot." Vehicles were crammed into every space often blocking each other in—but it was free. In November 1979, the University paved the area and made parking spaces for a student fee lot. It lasted one day. When protestors (sic), including City Mayor Gus Newport overwhelmed University Police and began tearing up the asphalt, the University withdrew all police presence from the park for several months. People set up tents and lived in the west end of the Park. All the asphalt on the westend was ripped up. You can still see the remnants of the asphalt mounds on the street sides of the west end. Trees and bushes were then planted throughout the west end of the Park. Several months later the winter rains drove away those living in the tents.

—UCPD History
http://police.berkeley.edu/about_UCPD/ucpdhistory.html

—Joe Mabel, Wikipedia, 1994

The University of California had pushed it too far this time. The afternoon before, a couple dozen members of their police force escorted a bulldozer into the park and began removing benches. The morning paper had written about a University administrative plan to start charging for the westend parking lot—the only remaining asphalt in the park. We had heard rumors about this possibility for months yet in the Council's negotiations with the University they insisted the rumors were lies. More bureaucrats speaking with forked tongues. The bulldozer was phase one. One of the park's denizens—a big mean guy named Tommy Trashcan—walked over to the dozer and pulled out the ignition wires. I never liked the fellow before or after that act, but at that moment he was my hero. The police attempted to arrest him as more cruisers arrived. After a twenty-minute tussle, Trashcan was in the police van. It was immediately surrounded by a couple dozen folks, who sat on the ground around the van. The cop at the wheel revved his engine and charged through the crowd. After that, somebody went to the tool shed in the bushes at the other end of the lot and brought out a couple of pickaxes. We took turns removing the asphalt in the parking lot piece by piece. After giving us a series of unheeded warnings the cops left, bragging to us that they would win and take the park back.

As the defining moment approached, Salty, a member of the park's organizing and maintenance committee, spoke on the phone to the mayor, Communist Party member Gus Newport. The Hog Farmers continued to distribute balloons. Somebody, maybe it was Wavy Gravy, was playing Reveille on a kazoo. Just as the riot squad moved into their attack formation and pulled down the clear plastic visors on their helmets, the mayor drove up. He got out of his car and waved good morning to the park's defenders. Then he told the police to leave. Since he was the city cops' boss they did so, cursing, one can be sure, the commie son of a bitch all the way back to their cars. This left a much-reduced force of University police who could do little but observe. Which they

37

did for six weeks.

During those six weeks the parking lot was removed piece by piece and the beginnings of a garden were put in place. The occupation of the park enjoyed tremendous support for the first month. The first couple weeks' worth of evenings, in fact, turned into big picnics with folks from all around the Bay Area bringing food, beer, pot and music makers. Merriment reigned those nights as people met new friends and hung out with old ones. Professionals with loosened ties on their way home from work joined together with hardened park habitués, musicians, college students and brothers from the streets of Oakland and West Berkeley and began to plant a garden where the parking lot had stood. Local businesses brought donations of plants and building supplies. As time went on, though, the picnics got smaller, and eventually the only people who remained were those who had nowhere else to go.... And those of us who still believed in the park's essential difference from the rest of America's "private property" and weren't too disillusioned for whatever reason, continued a public campaign in the park's behalf. Concerts were planned, agreements with the university penned, and gardens maintained.

—Ron Jacobs, May 23, 2003 www.counterpunch.org

—Jane Scheer

We must defend to the max the historic berms on the West End of People's Park. These raised planting mounds were erected with the blood, sweat, tears and blisters of the Park volunteers who tore up, raked up and piled up the asphalt chunks, rocks, roots and gravel from the University's parking lot pavement, for use as a barricade against intrusion by U.C. police and agents back in the heady days of the community occupation of the West End of the Park through November-December, 1979.

— David "Salty" Axelrod April 24-25, 2006

—courtesy David Axelrod

—Jane Scheer

—Jane Scheer

—David Axelrod   —David Axelrod

LANDMARKED

The Landmarks Preservation Commission, being fully advised, has voted to APPROVE the application to Declare the site commonly known as People's Park, a landmark for its historic and cultural importance to the City of Berkeley.   Dec. 14, 1984

You don't build buildings in parks for the same reason that you don't put up condominiums in the Grand Canyon. Soon you won't have it anymore.
                    —People's Park Committee of One. May 8, 1991

"I think that piece of property has a life of its own. In the long run, the people will guide its use."
            **—Andrew Youngmiester, a member of the Berkeley Landmarks Preservation Commission
                    after voting to name PP a historical and cultural landmark   Nov. 19, 1988**

People's Park is a City of Berkeley Landmark because of its important cultural significance. It is a living park under constant development by the users. This user-developed aspect is one of the significant reasons for its Landmark status.

                        **—Landmarks Preservation Commission-
                            Notice of Decision Aug. 19, 1991**

Section 3.24.210 of the Landmarks Preservation Ordinance requires that all proposals to demolish or alter Landmark buildings or sites be reviewed by the Landmarks Preservation Commission.

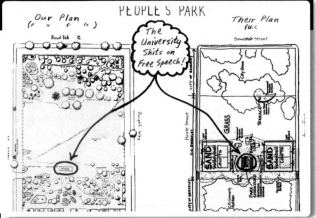

VOLLEY-BALLED

Protesters hold the Line —C. beck

A critical struggle for the land occured in 1991. The University, seemingly hoping history had been covered in enough dust, attempted to reclaim People's Park by volleyball. It didn't work. The dream of the park was still live enough to draw thousands together to prostest non user-developed volleyball courts that were put in with bulldozers and eight different police departments. In 1997, the university finally agreed to remove them. And a new generation of Park defenders was born.

In the spring of 1991, the institution of higher learning, the University of California, this champion of the first amendment, released its plan for People's Park. And what it called for was tearing out the free speech stage, in a park that's known around the world for free speech, and putting the toilet where the free speech stage was. So that forevermore people would defecate and urinate where there was free speech. You could put a toilet anywhere in that park but to put it where the stage was, showed the contempt that the university has for the first amendment.
**—David Nadel, March 12, 1993
recorded on Mama Oshay show**

The bulldozer arrived at 8 AM accompanied by dozens of riot police to break the ground for what will undoubtedly become the most expensive volleyball courts in history.
**—George Franklin
"Z" Magazine Dec. 1991**

I was opposed to the volleyball court because I really felt that the University put it there as sort of a nasty. It wasn't there for any legitimate reason...I started running up by the Clark Kerr campus and I saw the volleyball court there which was unused and the net was down and it suddenly dawned on me that this was ridiculous.
—Jim Chanin, interview Sept. 29, 2006

When I heard that the bulldozers were rolling into People's Park on Wed, July 31, I had to go see it myself...How to explain the sinking feeling in my gut, the rising anger flushing my face? As a 19-year-old freshman, I was one of the thousand or so who, one night in May 1972, threw themselves against the university's fence—the fence that had cut off the community from its park for three years. We tore it down, I always said, for the last time.

Back then the park meant so many things to so many people. It was a small zone outside of and opposing the existing order, the war, Nixon, and the university that supported it all. It didn't belong to the university, the city, or the state. It was the People's Park. That it couldn't last, an island of liberation surrounded by a sea of private property, of real estate, was inevitable.

But not because the community didn't try. Every time a park bench, a drinking fountain, a rest room, or children's play equipment blossomed, the university and its police were there to step on it, to squash the emergence of community accomplishment and transformation.

Since 1972 the university has fought a sniper war with the community, hoping the casualties would wear us down, gambling that Berkeley's shifting population would eventually erase the social memory of the park's importance, and planning to turn the community against the park.
**—Steve Stallone
*East Bay Guardian***

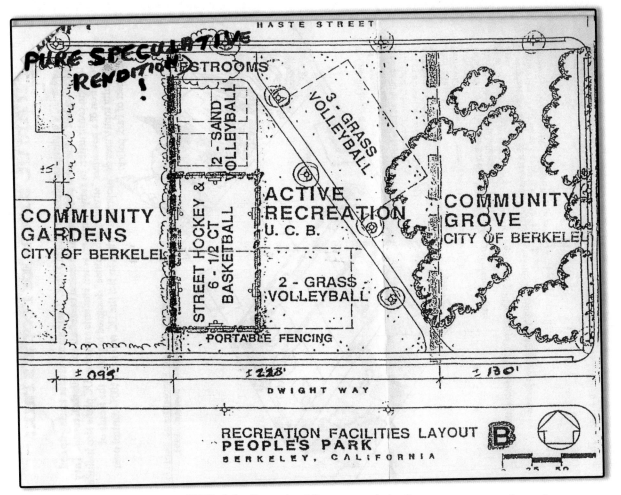

UC Berkeley Recreational Department design for sports courts, one of several

Protecting destruction — *Lydia Gans*

David Nadel chalking in defiance

The University of California is expected to begin building basketball and volleyball courts in the middle of People's Park this summer. This is after students have gone home, removing them as one source of resistance.

There is no known public outcry for more basketball and volleyball in Berkeley. The park plan is widely perceived as a device to drive homeless people, activists and the counterculture from the park by building stuff in their midst. ...At present, the constant presence of homeless people in People's Park is a constant reminder to university students, who one day will run our society, that their actions will have human consequences.

—**People's Park News, May 7, 1991**

Sweep the human debris from the park and demand that the university develop the land and watch the area become livable again.

—**Gerald Casey letter**
Oakland Tribune, Sept. 25, 1991

Meanwhile the least advantaged among us have this one little postage stamp of land where they can feel comfortable and at home—at least until the "majority" come along and say, "Move over, buddy, Dirk and Bree need a place to play volleyball."

—**Jerry Craig letter,**
East Bay Guardian Oct. 9, 1991

If volleyball players came to the Park and chose to involve themselves with the Park community and work together for a place to play that would be one thing. But having the University come in and build courts at no-ones request is a violation of user-development.

—**People's Park Emergency Bulletin,**
Friday Aug. 9, 1991

Nadel and other park activists say that any improvements to the park must be made by the primary users of the lot, and must not be "incompatible" with the the "founding" concept of the park." Nadel defined these concepts as maintaining the park as an open space, supporting user development, encouraging free speech, and retaining the homeless services provided in the area.

—**Daily Cal, Aug. 23, 1991**

The Rallyer

Free

June 20, 1991 Number 5

Feminism • Lesbian/Gay/Bi Rights • Environmentalism • Peace Activities • Ending Racism ...

Extensive Calendar of Events • Hotlines • Action Alerts • Grassroots Activism

SAVE OUR PARK

PUBLIC HEARING

THE BERKELEY PARKS AND RECREATION COMMISSION WILL BE HOLDING A PUBLIC HEARING REGARDING THE UNIVERSITY OF CALIFORNIA AND CITY OF BERKELEY PROPOSED DESIGN CONCEPTS FOR PEOPLE'S PARK.

THE HEARING WILL BE HELD AT THE NORTH BERKELEY SENIOR CENTER, 1901 HEARST STREET, BERKELEY, ON MONDAY, JUNE 3, 1991, STARTING AT 7:30 PM.

BERKELEY RESIDENTS WHO WISH TO SPEAK TO THE COMMISSION ARE URGED TO ATTEND THIS IMPORTANT MEETING.

Loni Hancock Speaks on People's Park

"You wouldn't build a volleyball court on the battlefield at Gettysburg. Our park's important so people can remember what happened there," she told a reporter on the 20th anniversary of the founding of People's Park.

- Sacramento Bee, SUNDAY July 14, 1991

The Peace and Justice Commission, having heard extensive comments from the public, and honoring the history of People's Park, strongly recommends that, in the spirit of the Human Rights Act, the City Council support the well thought out recommendations of the Parks and Recreation Commission; support changing the plan to removing the toilets to the periphery, providing for user developed recreation, protecting the constitutional rights of park users, retaining the stage at its present location, and retaining the Free Box for clothing and the Bulletin Board; and urges the City Council to ask the University to withdraw its proposal for volleyball courts.

—Monday, June 17, 1991, the members of The Peace and Justice Commission passed resolution by a vote of 9-0 [Ginger/Sherman]

"A user-developed peace settlement could be arranged," said People's Park Defense Union member David Nadel. "But the university has never been willing to negotiate with park supporters, so there will be a war."..."A park is a park," Michael Pachovas said. "It is not another Recreational Sports Facility."

—*Daily Cal* Aug. 23, 1991

City of Berkeley

LANDMARKS PRESERVATION COMMISSION
2180 MILVIA STREET
BERKELEY, CALIFORNIA 94704

(415) 644-6490

C I T Y   O F   B E R K E L E Y

N O T I C E   O F   D E C I S I O N

FOR MEETING OF: August 19, 1991

PROPERTY ADDRESS: Dwight Way, Bowditch and Haste Streets

Also Known As: PEOPLE'S PARK

OWNER OF PROPERTY: University of California
689 University Hall   Berkeley,   CA 94720

APPLICANT: Recreation and Parks Department, City of Berkeley
2180 Milvia Street, 3rd Floor, Berkeley, CA 94704

WHEREAS, a public hearing has been duly and regularly held upon the above property, and the Landmarks Preservation Commission, being fully advised, has voted to NOT APPROVE the application to construct restrooms/ storage facility, lighting, and pathways based on the following findings:

People's Park is a City of Berkeley Landmark because of its important cultural significance. It is a living park under constant development by the users. This user-developed aspect is one of the significant reasons for its Landmark status.

2. The plans presented to us have not involved the users and we therefore cannot approve them. Further, the plans presented, in particular for the bathrooms and lighting, would adversely affect the quality of the Landmark

3. Finally, the volleyball court constructed by the University since our last meeting was not presented to this commission and was completely out of the process. It did not include environmental review, which would have evaluated archaeological impacts. The City-University agreement should stipulate user approval for both City and University portions of the site.

NOW, THEREFORE, BE it Resolved by the Landmarks Preservation Commission of the City of Berkeley that the decision is deemed final unless it is reversed, upon appeal, by the Council of the City of Berkeley.

Motion Carried: Ayes: Bright, Cerny, Gordon, Grove, Kusmierski, Marsh, McGlibery; Rhodes; Starn.   Nay: 0; Abstain: 0, Absent: 0.

DATE NOTICE MAILED: 8/26/91   THE APPEAL PERIOD EXPIRES AT 5 PM: 9/12/91
FILE APPEAL WITH CITY CLERK BY THIS DATE

Bulletin Board on Haste　　　　　　*—Brenda Prager*

Getting arrested blocking the courts construction. David Nadel, Ben Fulcher, Bob Nichols, Susan Weed, Carol Denney, Jim Robinson, Michael Foot.　　　*—courtesy Jim Robinson*

Rebellion as volleyball court construction begins　*—C. beck*

Why we are opposed to University Construction.
This is NOT just a Volleyball Court

Sports facilities are simply the most convenient way to disrupt and suppress the activities in People's Park, and are not the result of a need for new facilities. The imposition of the sports courts, especially after all proposed courts have been completed, will:

1. Eliminate the open meadow character of the park that is essential for large, popular festivals and concerts, and conducive to frisbee, hackey-sack, large pow-wow gatherings, including religious services, and other lawn activities.

2. Create a difficult environment for current users of the park. Homeless people are treated like garbage throughout our society, and the operation of the sports courts will give the University police the excuse they want to expel or harass people in the park as "nuisances."

3. Simply restrict access to large portions of the park. The University plans to restrict access to the courts to students for the prime daylight hours, and charge for court use during the remaining hours...Disabling the Park's function as a resource for homeless people and people at risk of homelessness will increase the burden on the city and community to provide for the poor.

—People's Park Emergency Bulletin **Aug. 4, 1991**

People surround the construction　　　　*—Brenda Prager*

Activists feared that the building of volleyball courts struck at the heart of the park's traditional role—a place to "just be." As such, it portended ill for homeless park users and residents. It signaled a desire to see their removal. Reconstructing the park in such a way that would lead to the removal of the homeless, they surmised, was tantamount to an erosion of public space. The development of even volleyball courts had to be resisted...There was a lot more at stake in People's Park than volleyball. Most directly, as Duane, a homeless man who lived in the park put it, "This is about homelessness, and joblessness, and fighting oppression". It was, in other words, about rights, and about the right to the city. But such rights—to a home and job, and to freedom from oppression—were structured through a struggle over a right to and for public space, what such space means, and for whom it is "public."

— Don Mitchell, "The Right to the City: Social Justice and the Fight for Public Space", Guilford Press 2003

Holding the line

Police guard Volleyball Court   —*Brenda Prager*

—*Brenda Prager*

Keeping an eye on the "criminals"

Michael Pachovas gets arrested

On the morning of July 31, it was evident to everybody involved that Berkeley was about to explode. Attempts to break ground on the new volleyball courts that the University of California (UC) was planning to build on People's Park had already been repulsed by angry protests four days ago. Mayor Loni Hancock was literally on the other side of the planet—on a "fact-finding mission" in the farthest reaches of Siberia. The City Council was on summer break. Alameda County Sheriff Charles Plummer had already warned UC to delay construction in order to head off the impending disaster. But as hundreds of protesters gathered in the park that morning, a UC contracted construction crew arrived with their trucks and bulldozers. There were several arrests as protesters attempted to nonviolently blockade the 'dozer that started tearing into the turf just south of the park's stage.

Alameda County Sheriff Charles Plummer a veteran of the 1969 People's Park riots, told the Oakland Tribune that UC should wait for the situation to de-escalate before starting construction of the ball courts. "I'm concerned about the waste of money for law enforcement—all over a stupid playground."

**— Bill Weinberg,
"Berkeley's People's Park: Counterculture
landmark is once again Battleground"**
Downtown **(NYC paper) Oct. 1991**

C. beck

Getting an Education

Brenda Prager

The motorcycle meanies Telegraph and Haste

— C. beck

A university employee who asked not to be identified said that it was [UC Berkeley] Chancellor Chang-Lin Tien who had rejected the idea of negotiating any further over the future of the park. He personally rejected it on the grounds that he wanted violence and confrontation to show the regents he was tough. He [Tien] alluded to Bush's actions in the Persian Gulf; "you don't negotiate, you simply attack."

—**East Bay Express** Aug. 9, 1991

People's Park Battle Rage On: Police increase use of dummy bullets on protesters; Shirek calls for a "cease-fire"

The fourth day of protests over People's Park, which began with a peaceful march, ended in violence when two bottles were thrown and police opened fire with wood and rubber bullets on demonstrators. According to the police, 11 people were arrested, and three people were treated for minor injuries....More than 95 people have been arrested since Wednesday, when UC Berkeley began building two volleyball courts at the southern edge of the park.

—**David DeGusta and Geoff Ossias**
Daily Cal Aug. 5, 1991

Wild protests raged for the second night near the University of California campus yesterday until they were broken up by police firing rubber bullets into the shouting, dancing, bottle-throwing crowd.

Clashes between activists and police continued into the early morning hours. There were no police injuries reported, but a number of protesters and by-standers including San Francisco Examiner photographer Kim Komenich—were hit by the large, stinging rubber bullets.

—**"UC's Vietnam",**
Oakland Tribune Aug. 2, 1991

History repeats itself

— C. beck

Bonfire sports on Haste St.

Cops heading West on Haste St.

At last week's meeting of the Berkeley Police Review Commission, hundreds of angry park protesters implored the advisory board to take action on about two dozen allegations of excessive force.

—Daily Cal **Sept. 16, 1991**

U.C. POLICE
WE SEE BRUTALITY

From the back of David Nadel's boards

Shame on you.

**—Maudelle Shireck
to the university and our city manager**

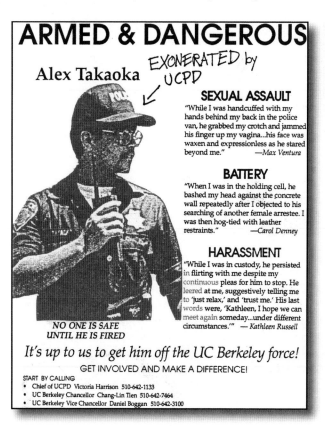

ARMED & DANGEROUS

Alex Takaoka   EXONERATED by UCPD

SEXUAL ASSAULT
"While I was handcuffed with my hands behind my back in the police van, he grabbed my crotch and jammed his finger up my vagina...his face was waxen and expressionless as he stared beyond me."   —*Max Ventura*

BATTERY
"When I was in the holding cell, he bashed my head against the concrete wall repeatedly after I objected to his searching of another female arrestee. I was then hog-tied with leather restraints."   —*Carol Denney*

HARASSMENT
"While I was in custody, he persisted in flirting with me despite my continuous pleas for him to stop. He leered at me, suggestively telling me to 'just relax,' and 'trust me.' His last words were, 'Kathleen, I hope we can meet again someday...under different circumstances.'" — *Kathleen Russell*

**NO ONE IS SAFE
UNTIL HE IS FIRED**

It's up to us to get him off the UC Berkeley force!

GET INVOLVED AND MAKE A DIFFERENCE!

START BY CALLING
• Chief of UCPD Victoria Harrison 510-642-1133
• UC Berkeley Chancellor Chang-Lin Tien 510-642-7464
• UC Berkeley Vice Chancellor Daniel Boggan 510-642-3100

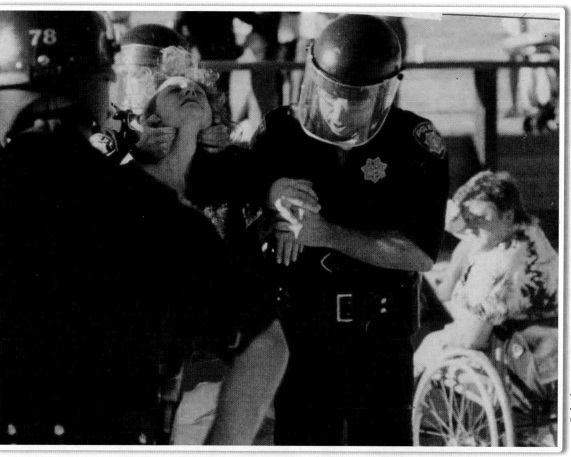

— C. beck

Danielle in a pain hold for volleyball

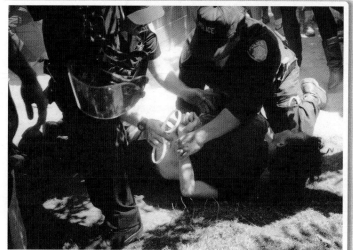

—Brenda Prager

— C. beck

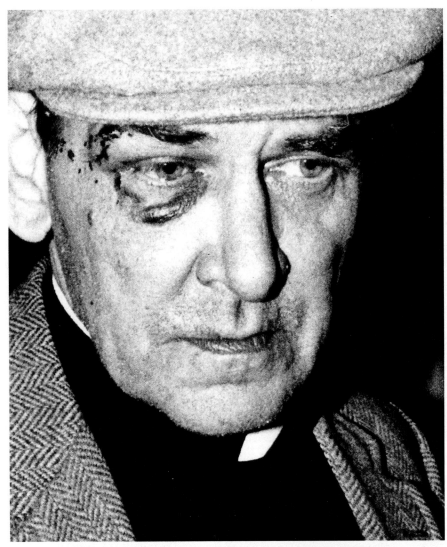

Priest hit in the face with a police wooden bullet during the protest

While the pair of volleyball courts now under construction are a part of the beginning, the City and U.C. are firmly agreed that much more will come. Under their joint agreement on the Park, the City will enhance the wooded and garden plot areas for public use, U.C. will add two more volleyball courts and an outdoor basketball court, and there will be joint installation of restrooms. Already, there are on-site coordinators at work to help bring a new spirit and assist in making the Park enjoyable.

We appeal to each member of the community to exercise every effort to restrain those who would provoke violence and to allow the development of People's Park to proceed peacefully. Each one of us must act as conscience and guardian of our community. That is the responsibility of a democracy, and especially in a community that values peace and the spirit of cooperation.

—Full page Paid advertisement in the *Daily Cal* Aug 2, 1991, Michael Brown, Berkeley City Manager and U.C. Chancellor, Chang-Lin Tien

"I really thought (the city and university) were on the same wavelength on going ahead with community involvement of the park," (Mayor) Hancock said. "The university decided too soon that (such involvement) wouldn't work."

— *Daily Cal* Aug. 22, 1991

"These are going to be the most expensive volleyball courts on earth," said Rebecca Rhine, spokesperson for the Telegraph Avenue Merchants Association, decrying the university's "unilateral decision" to bring bulldozers onto People's Park the day before. The university, she went on, "betrayed the trust of people who were suspicious (of the People's Park plan) to begin with."…"We're the battleground," she said, referring to the Telegraph Avenue merchants. "we're the victims here. The university is listening to no one."

—People's Park Chronicles, *East Bay Express* Aug. 9, 1991

"The Volleyball courts may be there for a while," says George Kalmar. "But if they try to put in another one, there's gonna be real trouble. Ultimately, they want to build dorms there. It isn't a business thing anymore. You don't spend $3 million to build volleyball courts if it's just a business decision. It's become an ego thing with them—as it has with us. Except that we're correct and they're not."

— Bill Weinberg, "Berkeley's People's Park" *Downtown* (NYC), 1991

I turn on the news and a newscaster intones, "People's Park has become a place for violent crime." Meanwhile on the screen is a picture of a man sleeping, his hat tilted over his face. This is crime? In my home town park people napped and they weren't charged with indecent sleeping in public. ...In the Park there is a large crowd, speakers not on the stage but standing one by one to talk. Everyone is in a circle and input is from anyone who wishes to speak, not just from leaders and well known activists.

—Carla Kandinsky, *Sacred River* Sept. 1991

At a Telegraph Avenue press conference, Councilmember Maudelle Shriek urged police to "stop the beatings, put your badges back on, and treat people like humans, not animals." She also urged that protesters stop the "trashings" and UC to stop the volleyball construction.

Council member Maudelle Shirek, outside Cody's Books on Telegraph Avenue, called for a cease-fi

BY TOM LEVY/THE CHRON...

Protesters and Cops standoff NW corner of Park   —*C. beck*

Tompkins Square Park in New York City, closed at the same time

To the People of Berkeley from the people of the lower east side, NYC:

Our parks are more than just trees, grass, and benches; they are monuments to the human spirit's thirst for freedom. The closing of Tompkins Square Park two months ago, and now the takeover of People's Park exposes a nationwide plan to eliminate public spaces where political dissent flourishes...Today we see fences around our beloved parks, but one day soon we will be selling the broken fragments of this fence in the same way that the German people did with the Berlin Wall

It's happenin' everywhere, places like Thompkins Square
Way over there in NYC
People's Park in Berkeley, Earth People's Park in Vermont
And Peace Park down in DC
It's all over the place, it's the law-they're up in our face
They're tryin' to put us down
So stand, stand strong, hold onto your heartsong
We can turn this thing around
—**through Ayr,
"The Parks are For the People".**

Most impressive about the uprisings in early August was the sincerity, the seriousness of the participants. The hundreds of People's Park defenders acted not as spare time activists, pursuing a hobby of feeling good for the day, but as actors upon the basic issues of human life. This created a village of resistance; a community of hundreds engaged in active, militant, daily resistance to the power of the state.
—*Slingshot*
December 1991

5pm meetings every day in the Park

MEMORIAL TO
CIVIL LIBERTIES
DEATH BY
VOLLEYBALL

Carol's Wreath Memorial —*Lydia Gans*

—*C. beck*

Nighttime resistance "business as usual"

Shitter toss lands in the
court sand —*C. beck*

the
**People's Park
Defense Union**
meets in
People's Park every
Sunday 4 p.m.
We need you!
Defend People's Park!

David Nadel flyer

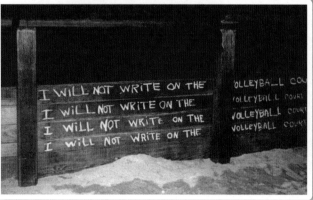

I WILL NOT WRITE ON THE VOLLEYBALL COU
I WILL NOT WRITE ON THE VOLLEYBALL COURT
I WILL NOT WRITE ON THE VOLLEYBALL COURT
I WILL NOT WRITE ON THE VOLLEYBALL COURT

"I will not write on the volleyball court" —*C. beck*

I see homeless
U.C. VOLLEYBALL

Altered billboard located at the intersection of
University and Shattuck Ave. in Berkeley

PEOPLE'S PARK, 1991

The university just built a volleyball court
on my youth. I watched.
The net was woven of my hair
when my hair was long enough to sit on.
The ball was my head
when my head bounced everywhere
and was never on my shoulders very long.
I know this happens to everyone.
Sometimes it's a department store
on top of a table where a candlelight dinner
is still going on.
Or a parking garage with a ghost tree
growing thru it
and someone waiting beside the tree,
still breathing hard because he ran all the way
and just got there
as Toyotas drive thru his side
and leave no wound.
Why should my youth be different than any other
just because it's mine?
I can feel the slaps on my young face
when the volleyball players hit their ball,
she isn't used to it.
Why are strangers beating on her?
She doesn't have any money.
The police shot at her, but that's different.
And then there's a crowd
and the police are shooting at us
and the bullets didn't get any older.
James Rector is the same age
as when they killed him 20 years ago.
Broken windows. Screams.
She can't believe this is happening.
I'm ashamed that I can.
I can't find anything to say to her,
not a single word.
This time there is no tear gas
to excuse my tears.

—Julia Vinograd 1991

—*C. beck*

David Nadel came out every weekend with his many sign boards and literature table, sharing important information with the community and publishing the monthly "UC Scandal Sheet"

Few were surprised then, that protests broke out on the morning the bulldozers returned to the park, slashing into that symbolic soil...Currently the sandy volleyball courts are guarded around the clock by police. During the first four days of construction, police protection for the area cost the university $32,000 a day, according to university officials.

"Over a dozen cops guarding a sandbox?" said Albany resident Shayna Levy, who had come one Sunday to see what was going on. "I can't believe my tax dollars are going to this."

"There was never a great need for volleyball courts," said Suzanne Pegas. "It was really the university trying to get the homeless out of the area."

"The university wants to make the park more respectable to new students," said student Alex Farr, who attended the protest on the first day of construction. "They've got a good excuse to build over the park and get rid of all the people who scare students. Students are afraid to see homelessness."

— **"No (People's) Parking Zone"**
San Francisco Guardian

UC Berkeley spent almost a million dollars to build a volleyball court in embattled People's Park and defend it against protesters. A series of protests cost UC $581,753 for private security and overtime pay for campus police, according to figures released by the university. The price tag for construction of the court came to more than $300,000. Another $66,000 was spent in legal fees to obtain a restraining order prohibiting vandalism in the park and defend a challenge against the environmental suitability of the project.

—*San Francisco Examiner* Mar. 26, 1992

Defending Volleyball   —*Brenda Prager*

Hateman   —*C. beck*

UC paid players $15/hr to make the courts seem used, and then paid for police chaparones.

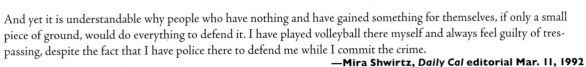

—*Brenda Prager*

Improper volleyball technique cause for arrest

—*Brenda Prager*

David Nadel & Carol Denney escorted off court

And yet it is understandable why people who have nothing and have gained something for themselves, if only a small piece of ground, would do everything to defend it. I have played volleyball there myself and always feel guilty of trespassing, despite the fact that I have police there to defend me while I commit the crime.

—Mira Shwirtz, *Daily Cal* editorial Mar. 11, 1992

Mural on North Haste detail

San Francisco Comicle
THE LARGEST DAILY CIRCULATION IN NORTHERN CALIFORNIA

7 ★★★★★   SATURDAY, OCTOBER 19, 1991   415-7

Playing volleyball at People's Park found to cause mutation!

NO EXIT   © '92 Andy Singer

U.Cisyphus

SINGER

...(DEVELOPING PEOPLE'S PARK.. FOR THE THIRD TIME)

BOYCOTT THE COURTS

Park Activists playing in the sand   —*Arthur Fonseca*

Sitting on the court   —*Lydia Gans*

55

This ball was hit out of the courts by some scab. The People's Team, the G&M All-Stars, liberated said ball, and used it for a quick game of People's Basketball. A real quick game. There were cops and scabs coming at them in a full park press right from the get-go. There was a scramble for the loose ball, the sister pounced on it, and passed it up park to the brother, who slam-dunked it into the shitter. A point well made. The cops called foul, of course, and brother Mike was taken away to the penalty box downtown...Mike's judge started laughing when the case was first explained to her.

She composed herself, but lost it again when she had to ask if anyone had retrieved the evidence yet. This case literally was laughed out of court. Case dismissed, charges dropped, something like that.

—"Save People's Park" C. beck 1992

Dunkshot in the Park's Porto-potty   —*Brenda Prager*

A game of taking down the nets

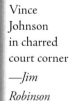

Vince Johnson in charred court corner
—*Jim Robinson*

—courtesy of Christopher McKinney

After a car landed in the courts

Garbage interrupts the game of scab volleyball

THE AMAZING CHAINSAW VOLLEYBALL PILLAR REMOVAL

An unidentified vandal used a chainsaw to cut down the central wooden post of the volleyball court at People's Park yesterday afternoon...The violent removal of the post followed a day of music and speeches at the park and two efforts by an angry crowd to pull the pole down with ropes...After a musical set by the local group Caribbean All-Stars, about 50 people went onto the court with a long rope. One man wearing a bandana over his face slipped a noose over the wooded pole. Scores of people gathered around the court to watch. Under the strain of at least 80 people pulling in an attempt to topple the pole, the rope broke. ... A second effort was made to pull down the pole, but the rope broke again. As people milled around the court, the sound of a chainsaw briefly filled the air and the pole suddenly toppled.

— Ian Finseth,
"Chainsaw ends uneasy People's Park calm" *Daily Cal* **Dec. 16, 1991**

Eli Yates lassos the pillar   —*C. beck*

The sound of a chainsaw gathers a crowd   —*Brenda Prager*

The middle pillar fallen. "Chainsaw Massacre",
—*C. beck*

The weapon   —*C. beck*

For those a little unclear on the concept of non-violence, ripping the center post out of the regent's volleyball court is not an act of violence, it is an act of healing. It is like removing an evil voo-doo needle from the heart of a symbol of democracy, of liberty.

— **C. beck**
"Save People's Park,
A work in progress"
1992

THE VOLLEYBALL COURTS COME OUT !

The bulldozer removes the sand   —*Lydia Gans*

Finally the obscenity is removed   —*Lydia Gans*

Tony, Russel and Moby give a thumbs up for court removal
—*Lydia Gans*

X-plicit Celebrators   —*courtesy of Debbie Moore*

"The protest of 1992 (sic) cost the city a million dollars," she (Berkeley City Council-member Dona Spring) said. "That was just for building a volleyball court. Can you imagine what would happen if the university tried to build structures? This is unconquered territory."

—*Daily Cal* April 11, 2000

"This never should have happened," said Berkeley activist Michael Pachovas, who was arrested in his wheelchair while trying to block the court's construction in 1991. "It was a waste of taxpayers' money to put this here and I'm delighted to see it go."

**—Jim Herron Zamora
"No more volleyball in
People's Park",
SF Examiner, Jan. 5, 1997**

AFTER VOLLEYBALL

A BENEFIT FOR ASHKENAZ DEFENSE COMMITTEE/SPEAKING TOUR

DAVID SLAPPs GOLIATH

—Zachary Ogen

Carol Denney, I came, I saw
www.caroldenney.com/slapp

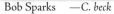

Bob Sparks —C. beck

David Nadel

The regents are also spending a ton of dough on their S.L.A.P.P.-suit against the People's Park 4. A S.L.A.P.P.-suit is a Strategic Lawsuit Against Public Participation. It is not designed to win any damages, or compensation for harm done; it is designed to intimidate people into giving up their rights to participate in our democratic process.

— C. beck "Save People's Park: A work in progress", 1992

In 1992, after six months of concerted effort to transform People's Park from free space to a UC and city controlled sports facility, the University of California tried a new tactic; a SLAPP-suit. SLAPP is an acronym for Strategic Lawsuit Against Public Participation.

Carol Denney was sued for more than a quarter of a million dollars as a "key leader" of the resistance along with David Nadel, Bob Sparks, Mike Lee, and 50 "Does", or unknown people in danger of being included in the suit through the process of legal discovery.

The University was forced to drop its damage claims but was awarded an injunction against the defendants which still stands today and threatens anyone who speaks against the University of California. All of Denney's named codefendants are now either deceased or out of state and can hardly pose a threat to the University of

California, the sixth largest nuclear weapons contractor in the world, which has spent half a million dollars suing Denney.

Denney was accused, among other things, of creating dozens of cardboard saws inscribed with the legend, "I came, I saw...", a stage prop used during a concert and demonstration in the summer of 1991.

Denney continues in her effort to vacate the injunction stifling free speech in People's Park. Any donations to the SLAPP-suit defense are greatly appreciated.

—www.caroldenney.com.

After the courts were rammed in with 500 cops, I said at a rally in the the park, "I don't encourage anyone to break the law, but I predict that these courts will be torn out as was the fence around the park in 1972 and as was the brand new UC parking lot in the Park in 1979". I looked back at history and I said, "well these courts would be torn out also".

Predictions are First Amendment protected. If you predict the sun is going to come up, you are not responsible for it, if you predict the Soviet Union is going to collapse, you are not responsible for it. So I made a prediction and

I've been sued in civil court in what is called a SLAPP suit, it It's an acronym for SLAPP which is Strategic Lawsuit Against Public Participation. This was coined by a professor at the University of Colorado, corporations use these kind of lawsuits to scare small folks from using their first amendment rights.

— David Nadel, recorded on Mama Oshay show KPFA March 12, 1993

I'm literally being sued for throwing roses into the sand and making cardboard saws.

— Carol Denny, recorded on Mama Oshay show KPFA March 12, 1993

—courtesy Kirk Lumpkin

Radical protestors during the 1991 riots included 19-year-old Rosebud Abigail Denovo ("RAD") (born Laura Marie Miller), a highly intelligent but psychologically troubled activist, who had previously been arrested and released after police found bomb making materials and an alleged "hit list" of university officials at a campsite she shared with a boyfriend in the Berkeley hills.

On August 25, 1992, Denovo, armed with a hunting knife and machete, broke into the residence of Chancellor Chang-Lin Tien on the UC Berkeley campus at 5:50 am. She triggered a silent alarm which summoned campus police, who escorted Tien and his wife safely off the premises. Police then entered the otherwise-empty house and shot and killed Denovo, who had allegedly lunged at an officer with a machete. The killing triggered further protests since the police entry was seen as unnecessary and contrary to customary police procedure (normal procedure when an armed, disturbed person is in a house but not endangering anyone is to negotiate with the person from outside). The officer who shot Denovo had just returned to duty after being wounded himself in a robbery, and he had also previously been the subject of citizen complaints including for excessive force, so the UCPD took further criticism for choosing to send an officer with such a history into the house.

—www.tvwiki.tv

Once they had Tien and his wife safely our of the mansion, the cops had a choice. They could call in a trained negotiator and talk her out, like they have been doing all week with those Neo-Nazis they have pinned down in Idaho. Or, they could send in some dogs and some shooters, and take advantage of this opportunity to kill her... The cops decided to send in a shooter who had just returned to duty, after being shot 5 times by a 15 yr. old robber. So even in the best case scenario, this cop was inclined to be operating on a shoot first, shoot to kill type of mode. Not to mention the 3 complaints he's had SUSTAINED against him while he was a Berkeley Cop.

They killed her without making a sincere effort to get her to surrender. They simply murdered little Rosebud....I'm afraid her spirit won't rest until we liberate People's Park. So I am definitely going to find a non-violent way to do just that. Then I can feel certain that she is resting in peace.
—C. beck "Save People's Park A work in progress", 1992

Rosebud Denovo was the victim of a political assassination. Once Tien & his wife were safely out of the house, the police had no reason to murder her!...If it was a preppy, yuppy student they would have called her parents.
—David Nadel

Rosebud's quiet, yet powerful presence will be missed at People's Park. So will her soft words and sweet smile. But her spirit will live on within each one of us who chooses defiance over oppression and injustice.
—Rose Shepherd

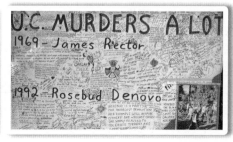

They had handcuffs on her and she was dead. And there's this question about did they put the handcuffs on her before they killed her, or did they put the handcuffs on after they killed her?
—Nancy Delaney about Rosebud, Claire Burch Video, 2008

Rosebud's actions were against a machine that makes war on all. Rosebud would have us continue as before. Thank you, Rosebud, you will never, ever be forgotten.
—John Vance

WHO OWNS THE PARK?

Someday a petty official will appear with a piece of paper, called a land title, which states that the University of California owns the land of the People's Park. Where did that piece of paper come from? What is it worth?

A long time ago the Costanoan Indians lived in the area now called Berkeley. They had no concept of land ownership. They believed that the land was under the care and guardianship of the people who used it and lived on it.

Catholic missionaries took the land away from the Indians. No agreements were made. No papers were signed. They ripped it off in the name of God.

The Mexican Government took the land away from the Church. The Mexican Government had guns and an army. God's word was not as strong.

The Mexican Government wanted to pretend that it was not the army that guaranteed them the land. They drew up some papers which said they legally owned it. No Indians signed those papers.

The Americans were not fooled by the papers. They had a stronger army than the Mexicans. They beat them in a war and took the land. Then they wrote some papers of their own and forced the Mexicans to sign them.

The American Government sold the land to some white settlers. The Government gave the settlers a piece of paper called a land title in exchange for some money. All this time there were still some Indians around who claimed the land. The American army killed most of them.

The piece of paper saying who owned the land was passed around among rich white men. Sometimes the white men were interested in taking care of the land. Usually they were just interested in making money. Finally some very rich men, who run the University of California, bought the land.

Immediately these men destroyed the houses that had been built on the land. The land went the way of so much other land in America—it became a parking lot.

We are building a park on the land. We will take care of it and guard it, in the spirit of the Costanoan Indians. When the University comes with its land title we will tell them: "Your land title is covered with blood. We won't touch it. Your people ripped off the land from the Indians a long time ago. If you want it back now, you will have to fight for it again."

Perhaps the most important aspect of People's Park is its claim to being Common Land. It holds the dream that there **is** land that is everyone's and we can share it. The concept itself is radical within a system of capitalism that has divided every inch of land and sold it to the highest bidder. Can there be a place where all are welcome and have "ownership" and responsibility to care for the land (and each other) together? Though the University holds a paper title, the Park has managed to elude control. It is like a tar baby. The more the University tries to assert control, the more resistance is mobilized to protect the spirit of the Park. People's Park is a struggle for real land. It is like land struggles everywhere, where people who tend and live on the land, try to resist control from afar and protect the life giving earth. It is a citizen resistance to the take-over of land by The Institution. It is the liberation from concrete of a small verdant oasis, an outpost from gentrified suburbia, a trophy from a dubiously successful uprising, a sanctuary for dreams, a ridicule of the dreams, an ember still glowing. The spirit of collectiveness and resistance lives on in the soil and our hearts.

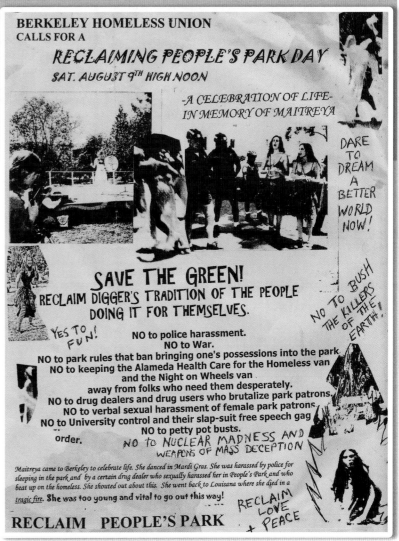

—Roy Williams, "People's Park Protest", May 16, 1969,
The Oakland Tribune Collection, the Oakland Museum of California. Gift of the ANG Newspapers

It was the only land in this country that no one owns,
and that's no small claim. **—Aaron Cometbus 1996**

People's Park

This is no man's land and no man
may profit from it.
You enter at your own risk
because the animals inside are not tame.
This
is ours,
whoever or whatever we are or aren't.
We don't have to get along, organize, explain
or be tidy.
It goes deeper and is much more simple;
we don't own anything except what we stand
up in
so this is a muscle we flex, a shared breath.
This is our skin, with flowers tattooed on it.

—Julia Vinograd, 1980

People's Park

The park is not loved because it is green,
sweet, peaceful and full of music
though this is nice when it happens,
good for cameras and historians.
The park is loved because it's ours.
When the park is full of garbage, drunks
and sad little fights, that no one wins
it's ours...
The park is loved because it's ours.
That's all.

—Julia Vinograd, 1990

A park liberated for use by the people is an alternative to a society dedicated to massive greed and the selfish pursuit of power. It keeps alive the rebellious spirit of the counterculture, when peace and love and justice were higher values than money and possessions and real estate. The most important thing to be saved was, of course, the village green itself, the commons belonging to all people.

**—Terry Messman,
"University of California's Disgraceful Attacks on the
Berkeley Free Box",** *Street Spirit,* **May 2006**

The long-simmering and sometimes white-hot controversies over People's Park in Berkeley are paradigmatic of the struggles that define the nature of "the public" and public space. Activists see places such as the park as places for representation. By taking public space, social movements represent themselves to larger audiences. Conversely, representatives of mainstream institutions argue that public spaces must be orderly and safe in order to function properly. These fundamentally opposing visions of public space clashed in the riots over People's Park in August 1991, and it is through such clashes that the actual nature of the right to the city is determined.

Spaces such as People's Park become, in Arendt's words, "small hidden islands of freedom". Such hidden islands are created when marginalized groups take space and use it to press their claims, to cry out for their rights. And that was precisely how activists understood their defense of People's Park in the face of the university's desire to transform and better control it. As the East Bay Express observed: "Ultimately, they claim, this is still a fight over territory. It is not just two volleyball courts; it's the whole issue of who has a rightful claim to the land."

For these activists, People's Park was a place where the rights of citizenship could be expanded to the most disenfranchised segment of contemporary American democracy: the homeless. People's Park provided the space for representing the legitimacy of homeless people within "the public".
...Like the streets of San Diego for the IWW 80 years earlier, People's Park was, for homeless people, a deeply political space.

—Don Mitchell, *The Right to the City: Social Justice and
the Fight for Public Space,* **Guilford Press 2003**

Today sacred space is seen to be sacred because of what happens within it and because of it to people—spiritually and physically. This means that our spaces must not only be places of communication and transcendence, which they must be, but they must also be places of incarnation. The hungry must be fed and the sick cared for. There must also be spaces which are free from oppressive government control and police harassment. There must be spaces which are distinguished from the homogeneous space of the city, the state, and the nation around them.

**—Gustav H. Schultz , University Lutheran Chapel,
"People's Park: The Rise and Fall (?) of a Religious Symbol"**

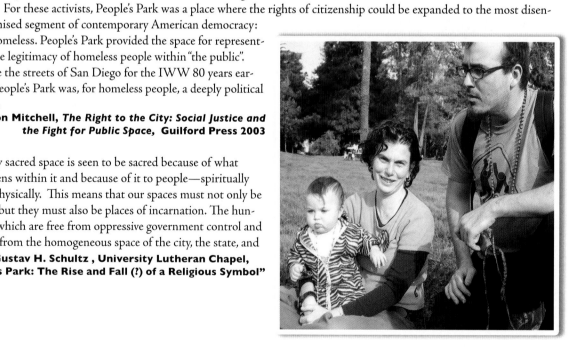

People's Park is not a symbol, it is a fact of life for the '60's, 70's, 80's and 90's. The park encompasses all the issues the movement has taken on over the last 22 years. People's Park is the environmental movement for urban land use of open space. People's Park is the movement for an open unrestricted public free speech arena. People's Park is the liberated zone of the nation's antiwar movement, opposing and resisting the University of California's perpetuation of the International Arms Race. People's Park embodies the anti-nuke movement with special emphasis on U.C.'s now defunct nuclear reactor and was the activist's rallying point for Diablo Canyon, 3-Mile Island and Seabrook demonstrations. People's Park embraces the movement for human rights and social justice, serving as a sanctuary, community service center, free housing and homeless rights activist and most important for the "Free World", it is the first line of defense against U.C. Berkeley's New World Order...The diverse street population of Telegraph Ave., the People's History Mural at Haste & Telegraph and People's Park are about all that's left of 25 years of radical direct action for serious and real social change. When south side is cleared of street people, hippies, punks, deadheads, rainbows, anarchists, radicals, Plop artists, political murals, free speech areas, street vendors, free clinics, food projects, Berkeley Inn site, drop-in centers, community and communal houses, and People's Park—the New World Order will have accomplished its goals.

—May 19th Organizing Committee (Bob Sparks), May 19, 1991

Since the early 1960's Peoples Park has been a contentious example of "the commons" in action. It originally proposed collective ownership and community contribution.

—www.delpesco.com/blog/

To me the crucial thing about it was the fact that it was not designed by a committee of suits and carried out in a bureaucratic fashion but that it was actually built by the people in the area who were going to use it. It grew out of people's own initiative and not out of some sort of bureaucratic plan. So it was the difference between the ruling elements in the state of California's bureaucratic plans for what to do with a piece of land versus a dream of direct participation in designing, planning and building a community....So then, pretty quickly it became a fight between those two things. And our view was that, you know, if you really looked at the land, just because the university said it owned it, what did that really mean? Because all the land in North America is ripped off, so we ripped it off back. So now it was back to a very clear kind of choice about who's side are you on. And because it was a park, that people enjoyed, and that they built, people were willing to fight for it.

...And they're still fighting for it, it's amazing. What is it 38 years later? It's amazing people are still fighting for it, it's quite beautiful.

— Frank Bardacke, interview Nov. 30, 2006

Do something special for our People's Park

People's Park needs You to do something nice!

Make Love with People's Park gardens.

Ask not what People's Park can do for you. Ask what you can do for the Park

Believe, believe in the Free Box!
Believe, believe in ancient oaks!
Believe, believe in People's Park!
Sunshine, Copwatch, local folks!

Save the commons, be a shaman
Everyday a new world's startin'
It's a good life in the garden
One where love is not forgotten

Drum those drums, make deep fun
Dwell in peace & peace will come
Drum those drums, throw 'way guns
Believe in peace and Food Not Bombs

Standing firm upon the berm
Every day the compost turns
Regents, change or ye shall learn
Karma's bad? Come back a worm!

And the peace in People's Park
Is a symbol & a spark
It's a place for change to start
'You see', a place for local hearts

Take a walk in People's Park
Smell the flowers, see the vines
Really good things got that glow
And they stand the test of time

Believe, believe in the Free Box!
Believe, believe in ancient oaks!
Believe, believe in People's Park!
Sunshine, Copwatch, local folks!

Martin's song Dec. 2006 .

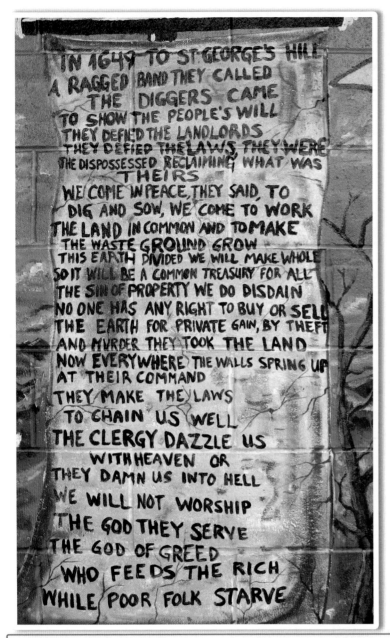

IN 1649 TO ST GEORGE'S HILL
A RAGGED BAND THEY CALLED
THE DIGGERS CAME
TO SHOW THE PEOPLE'S WILL
THEY DEFIED THE LANDLORDS
THEY DEFIED THE LAWS, THEY WERE
THE DISPOSSESSED RECLAIMING WHAT WAS
THEIRS
WE COME IN PEACE, THEY SAID, TO
DIG AND SOW, WE COME TO WORK
THE LAND IN COMMON AND TO MAKE
THE WASTE GROUND GROW
THIS EARTH DIVIDED WE WILL MAKE WHOLE
SO IT WILL BE A COMMON TREASURY FOR ALL
THE SIN OF PROPERTY WE DO DISDAIN
NO ONE HAS ANY RIGHT TO BUY OR SELL
THE EARTH FOR PRIVATE GAIN, BY THEFT
AND MURDER THEY TOOK THE LAND
NOW EVERYWHERE THE WALLS SPRING UP
AT THEIR COMMAND
THEY MAKE THE LAWS
TO CHAIN US WELL
THE CLERGY DAZZLE US
WITH HEAVEN OR
THEY DAMN US INTO HELL
WE WILL NOT WORSHIP
THE GOD THEY SERVE
THE GOD OF GREED
WHO FEEDS THE RICH
WHILE POOR FOLK STARVE

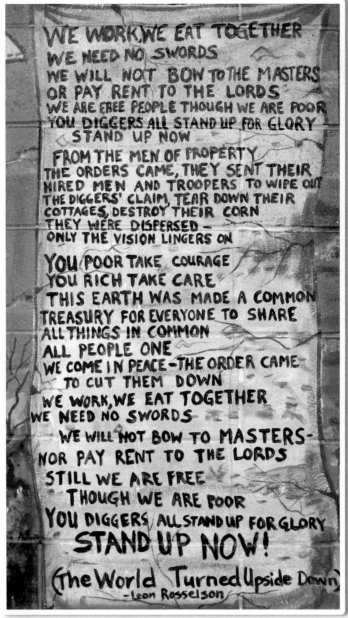

WE WORK, WE EAT TOGETHER
WE NEED NO SWORDS
WE WILL NOT BOW TO THE MASTERS
OR PAY RENT TO THE LORDS
WE ARE FREE PEOPLE THOUGH WE ARE POOR
YOU DIGGERS ALL STAND UP FOR GLORY
STAND UP NOW
FROM THE MEN OF PROPERTY
THE ORDERS CAME, THEY SENT THEIR
HIRED MEN AND TROOPERS TO WIPE OUT
THE DIGGERS' CLAIM, TEAR DOWN THEIR
COTTAGES, DESTROY THEIR CORN
THEY WERE DISPERSED —
ONLY THE VISION LINGERS ON

YOU POOR TAKE COURAGE
YOU RICH TAKE CARE
THIS EARTH WAS MADE A COMMON
TREASURY FOR EVERYONE TO SHARE
ALL THINGS IN COMMON
ALL PEOPLE ONE
WE COME IN PEACE - THE ORDER CAME
TO CUT THEM DOWN
WE WORK, WE EAT TOGETHER
WE NEED NO SWORDS
WE WILL NOT BOW TO MASTERS-
NOR PAY RENT TO THE LORDS
STILL WE ARE FREE
THOUGH WE ARE POOR
YOU DIGGERS ALL STAND UP FOR GLORY
STAND UP NOW!
(The World Turned Upside Down)
-Leon Rosselson

—Diggers' Song, "World Turned Upside Down", by Leon Rosselson. Painted on Park Bathroom Mural by Max Ventura, frequent singer of the song in the Park

—Below are new verses by Hungry Theater for their production of "World Turned Upside Down: A Tale of Two Histories", performed in the Park for People's Park 40th Anniversary Celebration.

In 1969 twixt Dwight and Haste,
A group of locals had a vision to create a public place
Where there was rubble, where there was mess
They made a people's park where all could come to rest

We come in peace, they said, to build a park
For free speech, free food, and love and to make a lasting mark
They towed the cars and planted trees
For three weeks they worked in solidarity

From Sacramento there came a plan
To use guns and chain link fences to destroy the people's land
Ol' Ronny sent in troops to stake his claim
Tear gas and bullets flew and a young man was slain.

We must take heed from this story
The land and water to grow food should not be private property
We have a people's park, but the fight goes on
Let's all stand up together, stand up now

—Hungry Theater

COMMUNITY GARDEN

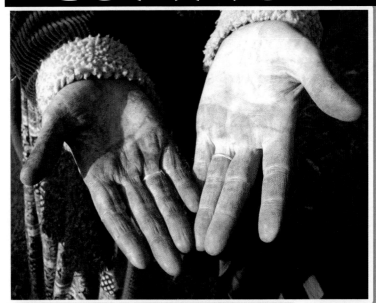

PEOPLE'S PARK

This is People's Park
where tattooed fighters planted rose tattoos
and roses grew
blood red.
It's not a peaceful place.
The vines are tangled with our nerves.
Grass untidy as a drunk's beard.
Trees grow shopping carts.
Bushes grow sleeping bags.
Lilies of the valley smoke cigarettes
they just bummed, but with such style.
Here are sunflowers that'll steal your backpack
when you're not looking,
daisies crooked as game booths at the circus
and violets sticking out
their impudent purple tongues.
Or is that us?
I don't know. It doesn't matter.
When people come to Berkeley
they always ask to see People's Park
and when I show it to them
they don't see it.
Next time
I'm not going to walk them a few blocks,
watch their faces and try to explain.
Instead, I'll show them my hands.
"Here's People's Park," I'll say.
"Here."

—Julia Vinograd, 1991

Gardening is what bonds us to the land. Where labor transforms into nourishment. Where seasons and cycles write change upon the landscape. Where miracles happen; seeds burst into life, baby birds hatch, compost happens, and people remember in their deepness where they are from. In some ways gardening is the essence of People's Park and the most real way we hold it.

—Crow

—courtesy Lisa Stephens

West End Community Garden site   —*Elihu Blotnick, Ramparts Aug. 1969*

David Axelrod

—*Roy Williams Oakland Tribune June 22, 1990*

And then there are the long-time habitues such as Lisa Stephens. When she looks out across the park she sees more than lawn, tree, and people. She sees ghosts. And futures. And, most of all, flowers.

A park activist for nearly two decades and one of the chief community gardeners there, Stephens knows every square foot of these 2.3 acres—and she knows the hopes, disappointments and passions that raged over each one. A stroll with her through the park on a sunny afternoon is a trip through that history, and a guide to monuments known only to the initiated.

"Here are Betsy's Roses, named after Betsy Johnson," she says, stopping before a small stand of red, white and sunset-orange blooms at the west end of the park. "everyone loved her, and for years she lived on the street on Tele-graph with her little pet dogs." Johnson planted the stand from cuttings. Since she died on the street of exposure in 1989, Stephens and others have watched over the flowers.

Nearby is the John Lennon Peace Garden, planted in 1985 in honor of the late rock star. At the other end is the Fred Cody Redwood Grove, named for the late founder of Cody's Books on Telegraph. Along Haste Street lies the "Peace Wall," a flower-and-shrub studded mound built from asphalt rubble torn up by 1979 protesters. A few paces away is a stand of trees called "Council Grove," where groups—such a Stephens' People's Park Project of about 30 community gardeners—hold meetings...

The park itself is like a plant, Stephens says: a continually changing organism that may lose a limb or go through hard times now and then. But with care, it grows—and makes others want to help it stay healthy. "Taking care of this park is about stewardship," Stephens says, waving a hand to take in Council Grove and the rest of the west end. "It's more than just taking care of the alyssum, poppies and cosmos on the Peace Wall. Its honoring the past, and remembering that the fight has always been the same. It's about who controls the ground. US." She stops, looks at her feet, then back up again. She beams. "The years go by, times change, but that never does," Stephens says, "And I don't think it ever will."

—San Francisco Examiner, Mar. 10, 1996

—David Axelrod

—Lydia Gans

71

The garden in the west end is a living testament of how paved and developed land can be reclaimed for life and nourishment, an example we would be wise to get busy replicating in many urban areas. Even with all the political and social issues played out in this place, it remains alive and changing. It provides habitat for many species, as well as air, food and beauty. The richness of the soil and the orchard are important emergency resources that would allow us to produce a decent amount of food on this land.

One needs to be somewhat detached to garden in People's Park. It is an unpredictable place. Some places have gophers or locusts...we have the University of California and wingnuts. I have countless tales, like the mowing of our artichoke patch by UC's workers. Also, unlike other gardens that may be fenced and carefully delineated, the Park is much looser with the beds and park areas all interspersed. The garden holds many delicious treasures. Come put your hands in the earth. The soil is rich and there's room for more gardeners!

—ed.

72

GARDENING FUN!
FREE SKOOL CLASSES
SUNDAYS 1:00 PM
PEOPLES PARK COMMUNITY GARDEN
(West End of Park)

garden. Attention will be given to growing patterns & native plants.

- Feb 23 Plant Walk (West East of Telegraph Ave between Haste & Dwight Street) Identify and discuss uses of plants, trees and weeds in the

Mar 2 Composting Learn the basics of successful home composting. Play with worms.

Mar 9 Peoples Park Community Garden Spring Groundbreaking Day Anyone interested in tending a plot should come out this day to claim one and to begin preparations (or call Terri 601-5673 or Lisa 845-7194)

Mar 16 Seeds & Soil Discuss issues of good seed and the growing crisis of diminishing crop species and the importance of home seed collecting. We will also discuss the basics of a healthy soil and methods to organically improve fertility.

Mar 23 Plant Uses A hands on discussion of medicinal and nutritional uses of plants. We will demonstrate various preparations of herbal medicines such as teas, salves and tinctures. (Bring clean small glass jars)

Mar 30 Sustainable Living This will be an overall discussion of how to live in a more ecologically sustainable manner. We will strive for a higher wisdom of possibilities as we discuss: alternative techniques for transportation, architecture, garbage, genetics, toxics and food. (This class will be held indoors at 3124 Shattuck Ave in case of rain)

April 6 Rain Date Classes canceled due to inclement weather will be rescheduled (Call Terri at (510) 601-5673 concerning cancellations and rescheduling)

—courtesy Lisa Stephens

—courtesy Lisa Stephens

73

Although people garden in the park throughout the week, most volunteers show up and pitch-in on Sundays. The People's Park Gardening Collective has now organized a series of gardening activities called Spring Sundays. Each Sunday from 1 to 4 p.m. through the end of May, Collective organizers will host a variety of workshops, with lessons in everything from composting to heirloom bean gardening. People's Park Community Garden Collective Coordinator Collette Mercier said these workshops are an effort to bring more people into the park. "It's a public garden," said Mercier. "This is a space where anyone can have access and anyone does."

Park activist and gardener George Franklin said that the community activism in the park's past makes it special. "I remember when this place was a parking lot and people came in with pick axes and turned it into a garden. We built every inch of this thing with our hands," he said. "I think People's Park is the most grassroots park in the Bay Area. It's a park that's been built from the ground up instead of by a park bureaucracy."

"I love this park," said Terri Compost. "It's just got such a nature about it. It's very much alive. I have gotten a lot from giving to this park."

—Tamara Keith, *Daily Planet* **Mar. 27, 2000**

Today People's Park is almost a model for any U.S. city: food is grown, there is a diversity of plant species as well as a diversity of people, some of whom live there (in the middle of the night the sleepers stay on the sidewalk where the police do not disturb them). This July Fourth I planted corn and beans there with friends, and noted the healthy state of fruit trees, berry bushes, vegetables, and herbs.

—Jan Lundberg
"Preparations and policies for
petrocollapse and climate distortion"
Culture Change **Letter July 8, 2005**

By similar reasoning, Planting Day on Sunday (second longest day of the year) afternoon is sure to be an organic gardening extravaganza... So be THERE and bust your assphalt...WELCOME BACK: Cowboy has returned from the interior...He is largely responsible for many recent landscape improvements to the Park's formerly desolate West End, along with Al, Bruce, Annie and other heroic volunteers....

— Ron and Salty,
People's Park Press Stringers,
DrumBeat from People's Park, **1982**

In 'Appetite for Change', his definitive account of how the sixties' counterculture changed the way we eat, historian Warren J. Belasco writes that the events in People's Park marked the "greening of the counter-culture, the pastoral turn that would lead to the commune movement in the countryside, to food co-ops and "guerilla capitalism," and, eventually, to the rise of organic agriculture and businesses like Whole Foods"....The organic garden planted in People's Park (soon imitated in urban lots across the country) was itself conceived of as a kind of scale model of a more cooperative society, a landscape of reconciliation that proposed to replace industrialism's attitude of conquest toward nature with a softer, more harmonious approach. A pastoral utopia in miniature, such a garden embraced not only the humans who tended and ate from it but "as many life kingdoms as possible," in the words of an early account of Berkeley's People's Gardens in an underground paper called "Good Times". The vegetables harvested from these plots, which were sometimes called "conspiracies of soil," would supply, in addition to wholesome calories, an "edible dynamic"—a "new medium through which people can relate to one another and their nourishment."

—Michael Pollan
"Omnivore's Dilemma", 2006

CALIFORNIA NATIVE PLANTS

Lisa Stephens

There are more California Native species (including endangered species) that have been planted—thanks in large part to Lisa Stephens who I appointed to the Parks and Recreation Commission...She is like an earth goddess who has worked tirelessly over the years to nurture the gardens and the people who come to relax in them. The vision of the founders of People's Park in the late sixties is coming to fruition. It is based on a cooperative way of life based on collective gardening, sharing of resources, and service to community.
—Dona Spring, Berkeley City Council Member

PEACE GARDEN

PLANTS

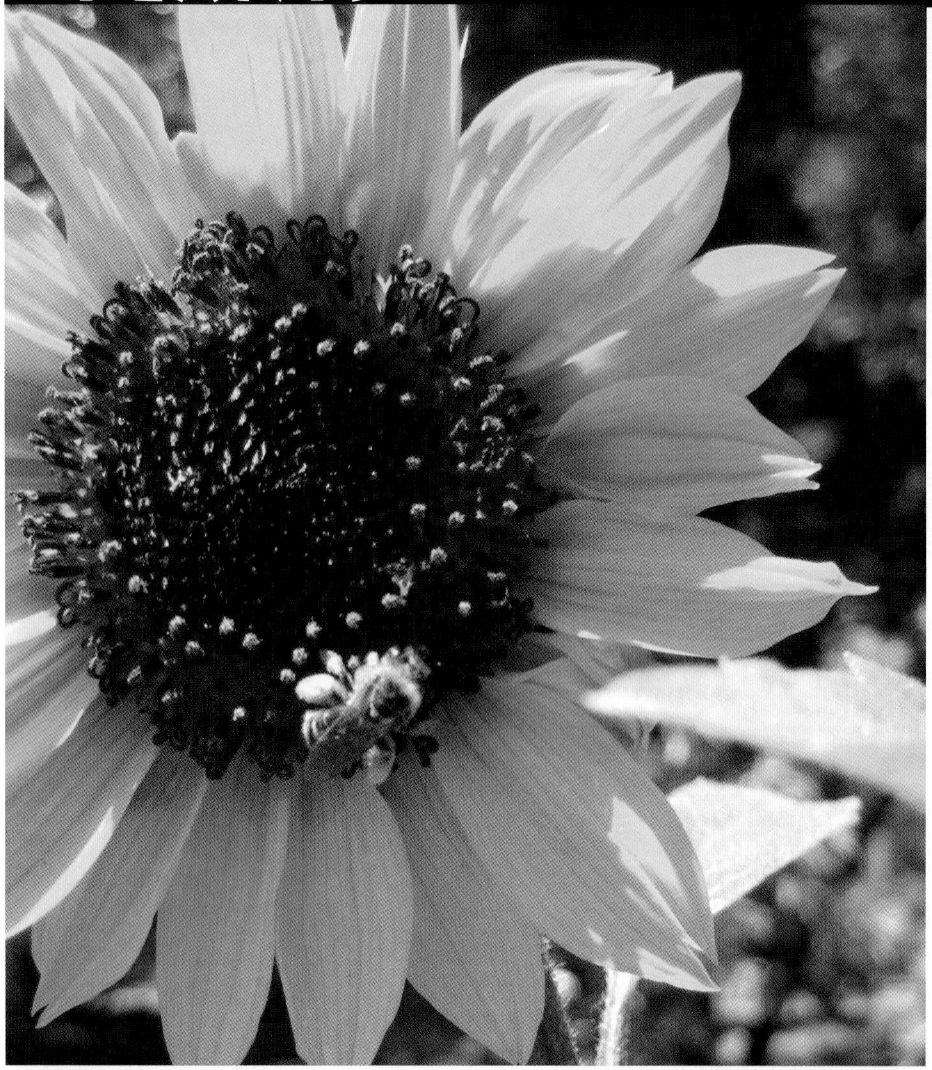

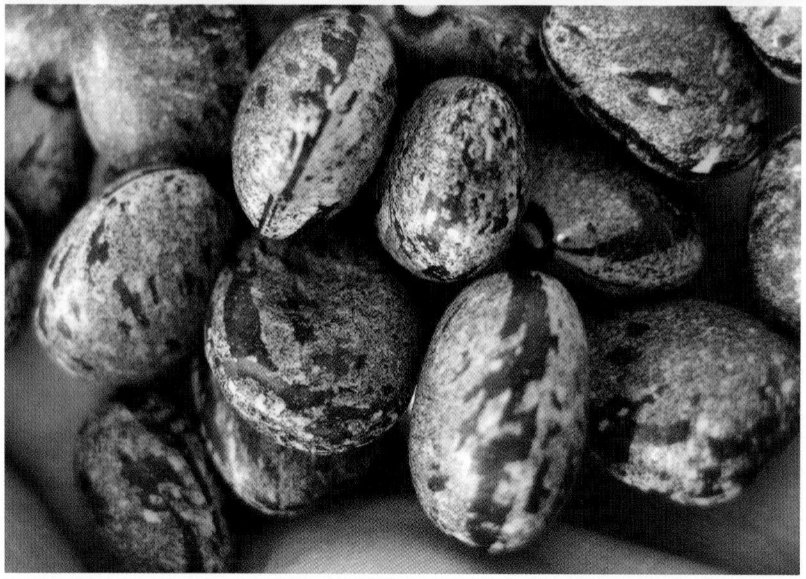

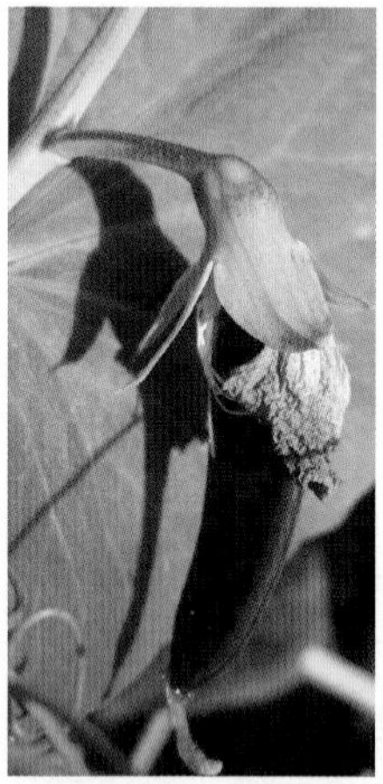

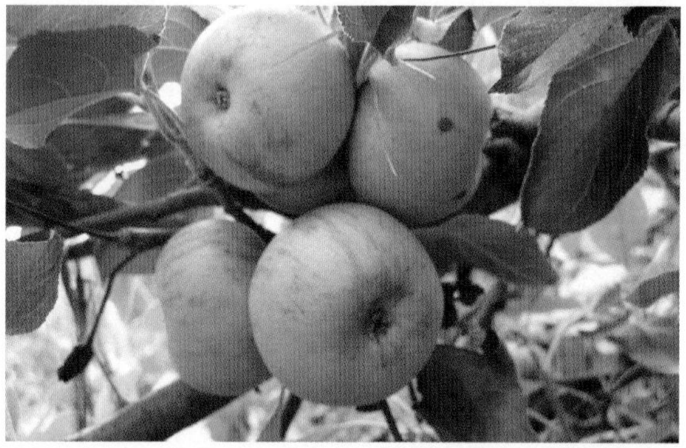

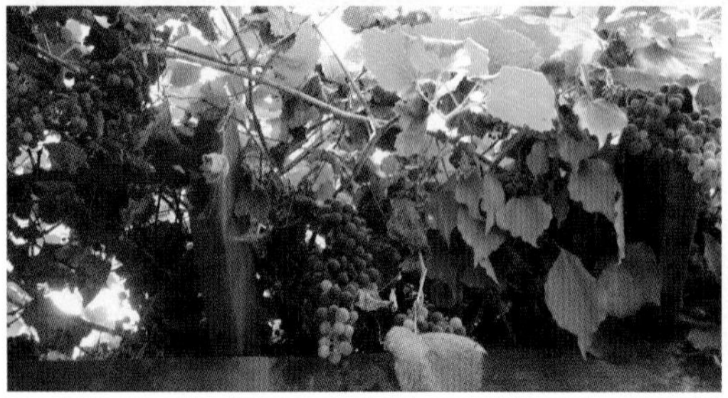

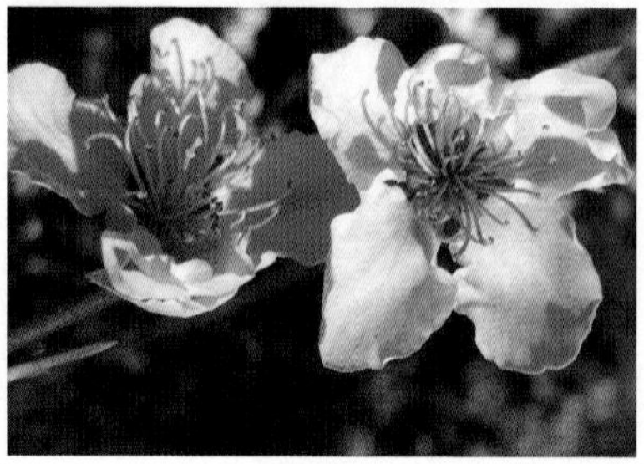

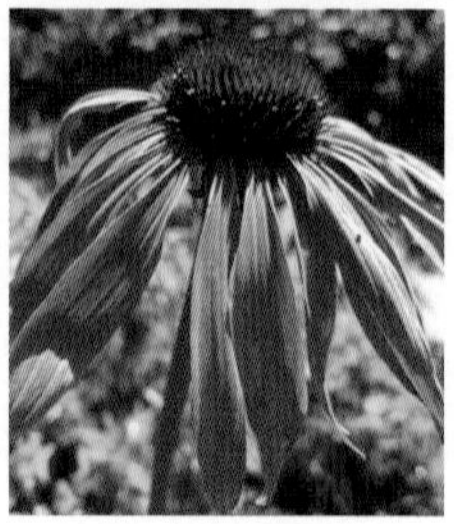

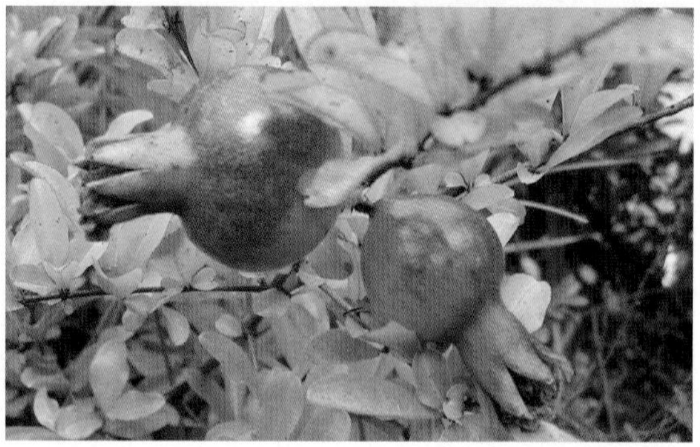

People's Park Plant List

Key: * = Still there in 2009,   n = native to california,   + = edible,   x = invasive

Veggies

carrots *+, parsley*+, cardoons*+, beets*+, sunchokes*+, garlic*+, lettuce*+, tomatoes*+, squash/ zuchinni*+, pumpkin+, spinach *+, sunflowers+, Brassica oleracea galore*+ (kale, collards, brusselsprouts, broccoli, cauliflower, cabbage), mustard*+, sesame*+, corn*+, artichoke+, asparagus+, chayote squash*+, nopales*+, onion grass*+x, fava beans+, MANY heirloom beans+, peas*+, potato*+, celery*+,

Fruit

rasperries*+, strawberries*+, kiwi*+, grapes*+, blackberries*+, pineapple quava*+, rhubarb*+

Trees

lemon*+, peach*+, almond*+, redwood*n, fig*+, willows*n, poplars*, cypress*, acacias*, walnut*+n, ash*, buckeye*+n, black locust*, monkey tree*, oaks*+n, redbud n, pomagranate*+, elm*, big leaf maple*n, plums*+, apples*+, crab apples*+, olives*+, palm*+, monterey pine*, Ironwood*n, oranges*+, mulberry*+, bay*n, inense cedar*n, birch*, dougfir*n, pears*+, nectarine+, apricot*+, loquat*+, avocado*+

Herbs (all with medicinal and/or culinary uses)

calendula*+, oregano*, thymes*, marjoram*, valerian *, St. John's wort*, mints: spearmint*, peppermint* chocolate mint*, bergamot mint*, lemon balm*, penny-royal*, lavender*, rosemary*, lemon verbena*,chamomile, sage*, vitex (chaste berry)*, mullein*, mugwort*, yarrow*, comfrey*, Jerusalem sage*+, borage*+, poke*, galium*+, lovage*+, fennel*+x, tansy*, fo ti*x, plantain*, nettle+, California poppy*, motherwort*, red clover*, echinacea*, elecampane*, epazote*, rue*, oregano*

Native California Plants

tule*+n, coffeberry*n, soaproot*n, silk tassel*n, twinberry*n, manzanitas*+n, butterfly bush*n, redwood sorrel *+n, matilja poppy n, red flowered salvias*n, wild ginger n, scarlet monkey flower n, alum roots n, prunus *n, ceonothuses*n, miners lettuce*+n, spice bush*n, elder*+n, horsetails*n, epilobium *n, dogwood*n

Flowers

roses*+, pin cushion*, iris*, poppies, angel trumpet, princess flower*, jasmine*, 4 o'clocks*, pansies+, hollyhock*+, periwinkle*, mallow tree*+, cala lily*, naked ladies*, daffodils*, hyacynths*, daisys, honeysuckle*, geraniums*, violets*+,nastertum*+,

Weeds

mallow*+x, sow thistle*+x, chickweed*+, purslane*+, scarlet pimpernel*, sour grass (oxalis)*+x, galiums*+x, south african daisy*x, docks*+, kikuya grass*x, bermuda grass*x, erharta grass *x

Other

bamboos*, cane*, prickly pear*+,agave*+x, pampass x, jade plant*, pyracantha*, flax*+, yucca*+, tobacco*
...   mushrooms, lichens, mosses, bacteria...animals...

What is User Development?

User development is a concept that was used to describe the creation of People's Park in 1969. Quite simply, it means that the development of the Park should be determined by those who use it and not by people who have never even been in the Park or who won't acknowledge the thousands of other people already using the Park.   **—David Nadel flyer circa 1991**

Environmentalist Alan Temko described it as "the most significant innovation in recreational design since the great public parks of the 19th and 20th Centuries". Also, Architect Sim Van der Ryn spoke of it as the forerunner of a new kind of environmental planning which would follow up user-generated design with community control. And as Sommer stated "...the idea of people designing and maintaining their own surroundings implies fundamental changes in the role of the designer and in the nature of the client."

—Robert Sommer's Design Awareness (1972)
Campus Ecologist, Summer 1983

The concept of paid contract workers implementing a design by "experts" that was commissioned by bureaucrats is completely against the nature and unique value of People's Park.   **—Sonnie Day,** *Slingshot*, **Jan. 24, 2008**

The People's Park battle was one of the first attempts to take the anti-war struggle from opposition and resistance to the realm of creating constructive alternatives to the problems of society. In so doing, the People's Park movement marked a transition from anti-war to environmental concerns.

—Text from History Flyer

Frank Bardacke states, "The reason they're so scared of the Park is precisely because of the way it was built; because their whole life depends upon the kind of structures where you have to have an architect draw up plans, and decisions made at the top that eventually trickle down to the bottom. So the reason they're afraid of this Park is precisely because people got together on their own and built something of their own...something beautiful and something creative; and that kind of thing, as far as they're concerned is very dangerous because we didn't go through channels. The reason they want us to go through channels is because that submits us to their control."

—People's Park Crisis Chronology
Armed Profits Affinity Group
For the Radical Student Union and the
Park Negotiating Committee
July 29, 1969

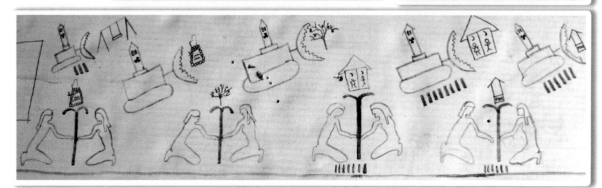

Hieroglyphic History of People's Park, explaining User Developed projects being destroyed by the University

So crackerman had a fig tree that had been in a 5 gal pot for 5 years that he had been trying to get rid of. I thought a great way to get rid of it would be to plant it in People's Park in Berkeley. Now, if you don't know the history of people's park, you should read it; it's very interesting. We loaded the fig into my car and started off on our safari. David is excited. So we stopped to pick up a third digger, Philip. After fueling up at Naan n Curry, we carried our tree over to the park. A really nice homeless woman named Mamma Dee suggested that we plant the tree where the cops had ripped out their freebox. It looked like a good spot, so we started digging the hole for our fig tree, now named Freebox Fig.

The ground was very hard, but we perservered with the help of Mamma D occasionally coming by to cheer us on. We dug....and dug....and dug. We were about halfway there when a bike cop showed up. He took our picture for the records and told us we were trespassing. It's illegal to dig holes in parks—even parks with community gardens in them. He told us that planting flowers or vegetables is entirely different than planting a fig tree. Mamma Dee stood behind us heckling the officer calling him "officer shawn don uranus" at one point...Anyways, he said we'd need to get permission and come back once we had it. Mamma D gave us all hugs and we filled up our hole and took Freebox Fig to its temporary home at Philip's house.

—http://community.livejournal.com

Rag-tag jugglers and clowns wandered through the capacity crowd that lounged on the grass, enjoying the mild weather and blue skies...In two last-minute compromises between the university and festival planners, the much-protested volleyball courts served as a sand castle lot for children, and local artists painted murals on the walls of the park bathrooms. "People's Park is the only community-controlled commons in Berkeley," said Dave (sic Bob) Sparks, one of the defense union's founders. "The recreational facilities of the university contribute to the destruction of that ideal." "This," Lisa Stephens said, indicating the basketball and volleyball facilities, "is not a compromise. It's the top-down, anti-democratic process that's been happening in all this development."

—Bill Draganza, "Park celebrates 23rd birthday", *Daily Cal* April 27, 1992

The land cries out for people to tend it, for people to tend it willingly and with love. It still is an open invitation waiting for that. **—Michael Rossman, Claire Burch video, "People's Park of Berkeley Then & Now"**

People Park Council (PPC), the park's democratic umbrella group, met for years as an unincorporated nonprofit association, (and a nominal member of Berkeley's Community Services United). The Council was a largely successful exercise in participatory democracy that arose from the design and construction of the People's Stage in April, 1979, and from the popular occupation of the West End of the Park during the Autumn of 1979. The Council, through its Operations Unit, was the vanguard of the struggle through the 1980s and beyond, insisting upon and exercising user development and community control of the People's Stage and of People's Park as a whole.

—David Axelrod

—John Jekabson

WORK PARTIES

Wanna paint the Playground in People's Park this Summer?

Let's get together & do it!

EVERYBODY GETS A BLISTER

—courtesy David Axelrod

The People's Stage, completed in April, 1979, had been designed and constructed through user-development and voluntary community participation, coordinated by the People's Park Council, a democratic group of park advocates, and the People's Park Project/ Native Plant Forum, a student and community group of gardeners and park volunteers sponsored by the Associated Students of the University of California (ASUC) and dedicated to the principles of user development and community control.

—David Axelrod, 2006

A work crew accompanied by UC Berkeley police ripped out the foundation for a permanent, but unauthorized, toilet at People's Park early yesterday... A group of park supporters— including some who helped found People's Park 20 years ago this spring—laid the foundation yesterday afternoon. They also dug a trench for a sewer line, which was filled in yesterday by a UC Berkeley crew... Michael Delacour, one of the park's founders, disagreed with that assessment. "They tore it out, we'll put it back," he said. **—Oakland Tribune, April 2, 1989**

People's Bathroom Destroyed

Another attempt to build a permanent bathroom by People's Park activists has been destroyed by the UC bulldozers earlier this week. This time they came in really quiet at 3:30am. It is the fifth time they destroyed the foundation for a permanent People's Park bathroom. At the moment, there are two disgustingly filthy Port-o-Potties to be used by approximately 200 people. This is clearly not satisfactory, we need permanent bathrooms in People's Park! Obviously, the University will destroy our attempts to build a bathroom over and over again unless we get organized and take over the park. If we had hundreds of people camping in the park, we could successfully defend the bathroom against the bulldozers coming in the early morning hours.

Slingshot, May 19, 1989

—C. beck

Eventually the University and City agreed to build a permanent bathroom, though this was protested for its prison-like design and the additional office. Activists feared the office would be used by UC personnel to monitor park activities and report to the police and dubbed the office the "cop shop". Eventually the much needed bathrooms were accepted after The People painted them with murals.

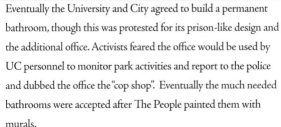

—courtesy Christopher McKinney

I think that the continuing idea that a piece of land would be cared for by an actual community of people rather than by a department of the city or the university, that's worth keeping it alive.

—Frank Bardacke, interview Nov. 30, 2006

People's Park Beautification

Join volunteers to make a special garden entrance in the southwest corner into the Park.

Garden Day
Sun Oct. 9
11am-4pm
Bring positive energy, friends, plants and tools.

Be the People of Peoples Park

Planning meeting Tues. Oct. 4, 7pm

PEOPLE'S PARK Kid's Page IS GROWING!

WHAT Do you want in your park? Write or draw here ?!

NAME
AGE

CIRCLE what you like

PLAY SCULPTURE   More Swings   SLIDE   Rope climb.

Donkey ride   Play ship   climbing wall   MERRY-GO-AROUND

THE PERGOLA

People's Park is built on the effort and ingenuity of people. That's the way the gardens and stage and free meals and free schools and free clinic and free concerts and free box were all created.

—Nancy Delaney
***Street Spirit* Feb. 1999**

Arthur Fonseca, one of the Park activists who has been responsible for carrying out many projects in People's Park, is in the process of developing a plan and working on getting funds and volunteers to help build a new and better free box. Arthur came to Berkeley in 1995 and got involved with Food Not Bombs. He recalls, "When I came to the park to serve, it was one of those things. It was a feeling in my heart that said that this is something that is incontrovertibly right going on here."

—Lydia Gans,
"The Radical Dream of a Space for All the People" ***Street Spirit*
May 2005**

—Michael Rossney Express Mar. 26, 1999

ART

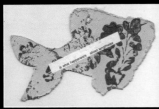

—Carol Denney

MEN   PEOPLE'S PARK   WOMEN

LET 1000 PARKS BLOOM!

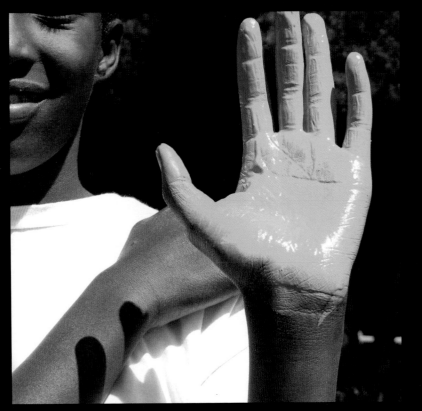

ART NOT WAR

—John Spicer

San Francisco Mime Troup   —Lydia Gans

—Elisa Smith

Art By Moby Theobald

Art by Charlie Williams

Murals on Bathroom in Park

—B.N. Duncan

He was playing on the sidewalk
For passing change
When something strange happened
Glory train passed through him
So he buried the coins he made
In People's Park
And went looking for a woman
To court and spark

— **Joni Mitchell**
"Court and Spark"

EARTH FIRST! LAST! ALWAYS!

88

Osha Neumann is a civil rights lawyer who has filed suits on behalf of the park's homeless people. He also helped paint the mural at the corner of Telegraph and Haste Street that chronicles the '60's student movement. On a recent afternoon, while he and fellow muralist Brian Thiele worked to restore the mural, he talked about the importance of the park to the memory of the free speech and antiwar movements. "The movement isn't as powerful, but the need for the movement is certainly as great as ever," he said. "The park remains a promise that it's going to come again."

—Angela Rowen, "Grass Roots"
San Francisco Bay Guardian

A People's Bicentennial History of Telegraph Avenue, 1976 (The People's Park Mural)

This mural was conceived by Osha Neumann and painted By Osha Neumann, O'Brien Thiele, Hannah Kransberg, Daniel Galvez and many other artists. The mural depicts the political and cultural history of Berkeley beginning with the Free Speech movement and continuing through the Third World Liberation Front struggle for ethnic studies at the university, the anti Vietnam war movement, the Black Panther Party and the creation of People's Park. The system against which the movement struggled is represented by the images of Richard Nixon and Clark Kerr, the chancellor of the University of California in Berkeley clinging to columns that have been torn from the administration building at the University. They are surrounded by a rain of television sets on which are depicted Ronald Reagan who was then governor of California, Lyndon Johnson, a Viet Cong soldier, and a soap commercial. To the right of this scene of the power structure in collapse, Hippies stroll on Telegraph Avenue. The People's Park Mural has been given the protection as a historic landmark by the Berkeley Landmarks Commission.

Osha Neumann and 1976 Haste St. Mural
—*courtesy Tristan Anderson*

—Mario Savio on 1976 Mural

89

In 1990, the mural was declared a Berkeley landmark, and this past summer the city allocated $10,000 to help restore it.

The mural is such a part of Berkeley's cultural history that we felt it was important to support its restoration.
**—Marc Weinstein,
owner of Amoeba Music**

Let A Thousand Parks Bloom
original dedicated October 1996
restored: November 2004
Painted by: Trish Tripp, Elvijo Dougherty, Edythe Boone
Assisted by: Robert Eggplant, Dave Salad, Sherman, Emily, Terri Compost, Ivy, Leon, Greg, Elisa, Stormy, Arinthia, Becky, Arthur, Tristan, Miranda and Jana

Mural on North Haste Street of Park in the 1990's

SHARING

—Lydia Gans

—Lydia Gans   —Judith Scheer

—Lydia Gans

—Moby Theobald

The "Free Box" is a clothes (and other materials) exchange. People leave what they no longer need for others to pick and choose as they please. The Free Box is a fully decommodified system of exchange of use values (to put it in technical terms), and as such represents the possibility of public space as a noncommodified space in the city where people can meet their needs in a manner not entirely predicated on capitalist relations of property, exploitation, and exchange value. Whatever the differences between the politics of protest and the politics of homelessness in the American city, they are united in their need for a public space either relatively free or liberated from the controlling power of the state and property.
—Don Mitchell, "The Right to the City: Social Justice and the Fight for Public Space" Guilford Press 2003

—Greg Jalbert

—Claire Burch

"It's something that ties the community together," said Dan McMullan, a volunteer from Friends of Peoples Park, a group that advocates for the park. "It offers the chance for an act of giving from people that have, to people that don't have, that makes both parties feel good."…When asked if he thought campus police would dismantle the freebox McMullan responded cheerfully, "Probably, but we'll just build another one."
—Timothy Martin, *Berkeley Daily Planet*, Nov. 15, 2005

Human greed is happening in American society at every level, including at the Free Box, but luckily the abundance helps a lot. Taking away services in the Park and the opportunity to make a little money might even increase crime…A Free Box builds self-esteem and equality between all comers. For someone on the bottom, nothing says more clearly that the people in the area care in a general way for all humanity.
—Nancy Delaney, *Street Spirit*, Feb. 1999

Free, like the library and a fruit tree. Free, like a little socialism to breech the chasms and schisms of capitalism's effects on community. Come unity, in a Free Box. The benefits outweigh the predicaments, in a Free Box. Power to the people property, like poetry stocks, free as the air you breathe and the water you see…You got a problem with the Free Box you got a problem with democracy… How many times have we heard this message before: because some people abuse the system, let's just drop it —not care anymore? Life is like a Free Box of chocolates, you never know what you gonna get or who's gonna get it. If people want to open up dey closets and dey wallets to help the needy, who are you to block it.
—Richard Moore, Free Box Poetry Contest

—courtesy Arthur Fonseca

—Lydia Gans

Praise the freebox in Berkeley which reduces the bore of wasting one's life in a clothing store.
If I give to the freebox I become free
of overconsumption's oppression of me.
—Joan Clair, Free Box Poetry Contest

Oh freebox!
Your very existence threatens the foundations of society…
That's why you're gone, for now.
—Maris Arnold, Free Box Poetry Contest

For the third time in as many months, UC Police have torn down the freebox at People's Park.
Volunteers erected a new steel free exchange bin on Nov. 12 after police dismantled a temporary structure to replace one damaged by fire earlier this year. Despite warnings from university officials that they would not allow a new freebox at the park, supporters were hopeful that the new box would last…But those hopes were dashed as police entered the park under the cover of darkness early Wednesday morning to dismantle the eight-by-four foot metal structure.
—Timothy Martin, *Berkeley Daily Planet*, Jan. 27, 2006

For many of its supporters, the free box is emblematic of a time when people gave a damn about social injustice and the ideals of brotherhood and sisterhood. People's Park lives as a concrete expression of the values of sharing, community and freedom…What is at stake in the struggle over the free box is the very soul of People's Park and the very concept of the village green.
—Terry Messman, *Street Spirit*, May 2006

The People's Park in Berkeley may be losing its "Free Box"—where old possessions can be cast off in a good-karma way, and disturbing bums can fight over the right to take the stuff and sell it. Both Town, as represented by the Telegraph Business Improvement District, and Gown, represented by U-Cal Berkeley, want it gone. However, if the hippies keep rebuilding it, well, it will still be there. Until it gets torn down, burned down, or stolen. It's apparently a veritable endless twisting mandala of karmic action and reaction, as well as a place to fight with people of dubious if not frightening hygiene over old shoes.
— Brian Doherty, www.reason.com April 26, 2006

People's Park, a Berkeley landmark, has a tradition of free exchange. The tradition of sharing food, sharing music, trading clothing, giving away helpful information (and yes, sometimes love) without compensation is more than 35 years old. The freebox, one of the best examples of this tradition, is simply a box into which one puts old or simply unwanted items for the next person to use, and takes whatever interests them…The absence of the freebox for the last six months didn't cure the world of selfishness or drug abuse, if that's what the university thought would happen, so there's no need to deprive the park of its traditions. The answer to selfishness might be more, rather than less, freeboxes.
—Carol Denney, "10 Myths about the Freebox", *Berkeley Daily Planet*, Oct. 25, 2005

SAVE THE FREEBOX

The university refuses to recognize the long-standing tradition of free exchange in People's Park, and has forgotten the compromise agreement made with free box advocates in 1998 when the university itself moved the activist-built freebox to its most recent location.

—Arthur Fonseca, *Daily Planet*, Dec. 13, 2005

The University of California administration destroyed our free clothing box in People's Park, sneakily, in the dark. Like criminals, they stole a very important resource for sharing in our community.... Why? Irene Hegarty, from UC's Community Relations Department says, "People have taken the clothes and sold them to buy drugs or alcohol...It just has not been a productive way to get clothes to homeless people." First off, in fact, the freebox is an active and effective distribution system, getting clothes to many people. It's open 24 hours a day and it costs nothing. It certainly is a more "productive" way of getting clothes to the homeless than removing the box and throwing away the clothes as UC has been doing...Secondly, the complaint about people selling the clothes is absurd. Who cares if someone sells something? It was given to them, it's legal and there is plenty to go around. It is actually a great skill and service if one can identify clothes that are fashionable enough to be bought. That allows college students better prices at the used clothing stores and helps those local businesses. It reduces societal consumption. And why is it assumed that if a poor person makes money it is for "drugs or alcohol"?

—Terri Compost, *Daily Planet*, Nov. 29, 2005

(to the right)

People's Park "Free Rocks", the new way clothes are distributed without the box. Get 'um before they are thrown in the dumpster!

—Lydia Gans   *—courtesy IndyBay*

Our sturdy wooden Freebox was burned. The culprit was never found. In November of 2005 we built another lovely metal one, that was removed within days by the University in the middle of the night. As of April 2009, clothes are being distributed on the "Free Rocks", as the community still cares to share and the clothes are needed more than ever.

—ed.

As an ongoing effort, New Church has organized a group of folks on Saturday mornings to make bag lunches for those in People's Park. Most of the time the lunches go pretty quickly! According to the men and women who receive the lunches, the clean white socks are the best treat. Sometimes there are folks who want to chat for a while, and every now and then we meet someone who wants to come to church. This is a great way to just show grace to the people of Berkeley and to stay in touch with how hard life is when you're homeless.

—www.newchurchberkeley.org

"Dear friend, we towed a building onto People's Park this morning and opened for breakfast as People's Cafe—the Berkeley Catholic Worker House of Hospitality. We'd like to explain our action and ask for your support."

—Letter to Berkeley Catholic Worker supporters

—Daily Cal May 10, 1989

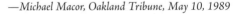

—Michael Macor, Oakland Tribune, May 10, 1989

About five minutes after the load had been dumped and the truck had been driven away, a group of UC police officers arrived on the scene. "They didn't make any attempt to get us to move it," says (John) Cooper. "A lieutenant looked at the tires and said, "You let the air out of the tires, did you?" And I said, 'Yes sir.' And then he looked at them again and looked up at me and said, 'And after that, did you slash the tires?' And I said, 'I'm afraid we did' And to do him credit, he looked at me and smiled slightly, in understanding.

—Mike McGrath, "The Arrival of People's Cafe"
East Bay Express, May 26, 1989

J.C. Horton and Catholic Worker Lunch   *—Lydia Gans*

Recognize the presence of the Berkeley Catholic Worker People's Cafe as a positive interim development and support its present site in People's Park while other sites are explored.

—City Council minutes June 6, 1989,
Moved, seconded, carried (Jelinek)

The Catholic Worker's People's Cafe, a 66 foot trailer towed onto the park on May 9th is still serving breakfast every morning, and is open from 7-12 am. Most people in the Park are very pleased with the new cafe and appreciate the Catholic Worker's action. But there are others who are upset because they oppose any building on People's Park.

— "People's Cafe Stays in Park", Slingshot, May 19, 1989

You got here and the homeless people would be having coffee and croissants and sitting there in the fresh air and it was beautiful. Suddenly at breakfast time the park was transformed. It was really like a cafe. And then I guess UC ditched it. I was very pissed. I thought, "What a beautiful custom". It did nobody any harm. The Dorothy Day people—it was charming. And boom, it was gone.

—Claire Burch interview, Feb. 28, 2007

—courtesy Lisa Stephens

—Pierre La Plant

—Stephen Shames

Berkeley Farmer's Market
on Haste Street
—courtesy Kirk Lumpkin

—Lydia Gans

96

FOOD NOT BOMBS

East Bay Food Not Bombs formed in 1991, and has been serving free vegetarian lunches in People's Park every weekday since (at 3pm). The all volunteer run organization has substantially nourished community in the Park.

—Rosevelt Stephens

—Lydia Gans

—art by Guy Colwell

—Lydia Gans

97

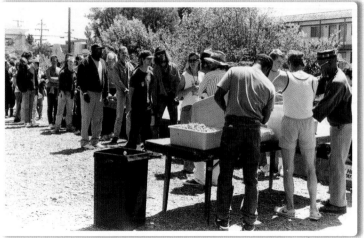

—Lydia Gans   —Lydia Gans

Food Not Bombs is like the signature of the park. It's not like the dreary soup kitchens, it's cheerful.
—Claire Burch interview, Feb. 28, 2007

This creation of community, of peaceful space, is our most important "service" and is why we stay in the park. All over the world it is understood that to break bread with another is to recognize him/her as a fellow human being.
—Judy Foster about Food Not Bombs,
East Bay Express, Sept. 15, 1995

Oh, and I guess Food not Bombs is even criminalized by the cops—for leaving a mess in the park or something?

Hmm, I don't buy it. I've only been to two Food Not Bombs lunches at the park, but neither of them left a trail of delicious biodegradable vegetarian scraps in their wake. And anyway, if there was some litter, does that merit police harrass-

—Lydia Gans

ment? (Does anything?) The benefits of feeding hungry people surely outweigh any negative effects!
—fridayinluv.livejournal.com

Excerpts from *East Bay Food Not Bombs*, 2000

East Bay Food Not Bombs' history is inextricably linked to People's Park...As long as we continue to come together in solidarity and defend the park and its purpose—as a place where ALL people are able to gather to meet the needs of the body, to rest, to have access to open space, to be able to eat and clothe oneself, meet others, build community, and finally, unite in resistance and attempt to create a viable alternative to the oppressive nature of capitalist society—the university will have a formidable opponent in this struggle in and over what is truly public space....We cook and serve to anyone who cares to eat, including each other—not as an act of charity, but to empower as well as nourish. We succeed in a modest way. The best you can do in these terrible times (the Kali Yuga, some call it) is to hold on to each other and work for change.
—Judy Foster

Food Not Bombs is community. Five days a week I can

—Crow

head to People's Park and get a filling, healthy meal. I help out when I can, and when I can't, other people fill in the blanks. But somehow the meal appears, and FNB keeps chugging along. All sorts of people helping each other.
—Marcus

People would wind up in the Park looking for something, With our hopes, needs, problems, desperation, political ideas and mainly, with our desire to be with other people, connected in some way...Then Stephen told me about Food Not Bombs starting and soon I got involved. No matter how scattered the scene around the Park would get at least there would always be food, a tangible, constant thing, bringing us back down to earth.
—Elisa

Its good for people to work together for a common altruistic goal. It is our practical prayer that no one will go hungry today... we can't live without community.
—Arthur

—Lydia Gans

REFUGE

The Park is frightening and wondrous. We have seen it now at dawn, on a sunny afternoon, at midnight. Clusters, individuals, move through the trees, across the grass, in harmony, in conflict, united in raw, un-bridled humaness. A dog jumps to snatch a frisbee. People cheer—it is a Park dog. Pops is out of jail today. Chicken George got out last week—guileless innocents, children of God. Some folk are gentle, a few are warlike. Some have criminal records for doing, perforce in pub-lic, what others do at home. People talking to people, to themselves, to no one. People celebrating God, oblivious to God, people whom God has deserted, this is People's Park. Those who have eyes to see, let them.
—John Delmos, Catholic Worker Pamphlet

Spending time at People's Park erased some of its mystic for me, but it gave me a better understanding of why it is important. Not because it is a symbol of the 60s, but because it adds a little comfort to the lives of many people who have little else. It is a green refuge with shade and grass in a crowded and congested little city.
—May 18, 1994 A collection of opinions collected by Tom Leon-ard for the "City of Berkeley /University of California /People's Park 1993-94 Annual Evaluation"

People's Park has always supported and given refuge to those in mental crises.
—Kat and Michael Diehl, Humane Services for the Mentally Crisesed, June 26, 2009

People's Park isn't always a place to get peace and quiet, that's for damn sure. There'll be people yelling and going off, y'know. But sometimes it's a real peaceful place.
—John Delmos, interviews in 1993 and 1994 by B.N Duncan

99

SURVIVAL UNDER CAPITALISM

It's 7 a.m. in People's Park and a woman blow-drying her socks in the public restroom is staging a revolution of her own. "UC scum! Do you even know what this park means?" Deborah screams at no one in particular.

—Jessica Meyers, J200 class, Sept. 12, 2006

I think People's Park means freedom: a place where people can go and relax, and not worry about the police, and not worry about the people bumping into them as they walk by. Where they can set down their backpacks, and play cards, and relax in the sun, and enjoy the weather, and commune with nature....Whereas on the cement, all you do, you have to walk around because if you don't they'll call it loitering.

— Narayana "People's Park Speak-Out" B.N Duncan interviews in 1993 and 1994

True, People's Park does have an aesthetic value as a sort of living museum to social failure....

—Brook Schaaf, *Daily Cal* Mar. 3, 2000

Pundits on the right often cite People's Park as the personification of the "People's Republic of Berkeley". Capitalists hate People's Park, because it represents a living example of public defiance against the iron laws of the "free market" and their near hysterical sacred cow of "private property". ...The Bay Area IWW's history is intertwined with The History of People's Park. Many of those who originally created People's Park were (at least partly) influenced by the history of the Wobblies of old. The riots that took place in the 1990s (caused at least as much by the University and dozens of police departments that invaded Berkeley at that time as Park supporters) brought SLAPP suits against four activists, one of whom (Bob Sparks) was a dues paying Wobbly. In 1995, the Bay Area IWW celebrated the 90th Anniversary of its founding convention in People's Park (during the People's Park's own anniversary celebration.)

—"Capitalism— not People's Park— killed Cody's Books" www.retailworker.com

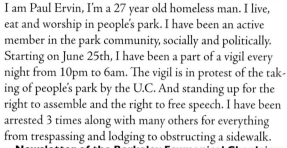

I am Paul Ervin, I'm a 27 year old homeless man. I live, eat and worship in people's park. I have been an active member in the park community, socially and politically. Starting on June 25th, I have been a part of a vigil every night from 10pm to 6am. The vigil is in protest of the taking of people's park by the U.C. And standing up for the right to assemble and the right to free speech. I have been arrested 3 times along with many others for everything from trespassing and lodging to obstructing a sidewalk.

—Newsletter of the Berkeley Ecumenical Chaplaincy to the Homeless *Homeless Voice*, 1991

Brad Picard, landscape architect with the City of Berkeley Parks, Recreation and Waterfront Department, has worked with some of the Park activist volunteers. "It has a style and energy all its own," he notes..."It's incredible the impact it can absorb," he enthuses. "And it's got history, very rich significance. A tiny little park. It's just amazing to me. I've always thought it's one of the healthiest parks I've ever seen."

—Lydia Gans, "The Radical Dream of a Space for All the People", *Street Spirit* July 2005

Memo to self: If I ever become a hopeless crack addict, this is one of the more scenic places to score.

—Benjamin J., Yelp April 13, 2008

People's Park is an area for people without money and power to hang out and live during the day, and maybe even find refuge.
People's Park is an area where poor and broke people can get free food, and free clothing.
People's Park is an area where some poor and broke people have gotten medical and dental treatment through special service.
People's Park is an area for drinking and drug-dealing and drug-taking.
People's Park is an area for anti-social people to mess around and get away with it when they wouldn't get away with it some place else.
People's Park is an area for recreational activity.
People's Park is an area for the peaceful, positive work of gardening.

—Roosevelt Stephens

People's Park is an area for artists to convey messages.
People's Park is an area for shows and entertainment and oratory, and significant communication for mind and spirit.
People's Park is an area for some people to take part in their religion.
People's Park is an area where some people hold weddings.
People's Park is an area where some people honor their dead.
People's Park is an area where some people of various walks of life look for unity and amity and fulfillment together in a largely artificial, divided, alienation-producing society.
People's Park is an area of defiance to tyranny and the mechanical-dominated, bureacratic-dominated, elitist established order of society.
People's Park is an area of nature and leisure that's a relief from much of urban conditions.

—B.N. Duncan, 1994

I'm tired of the People's Park being blamed for society's problems, and having those in turn be characterized as "public safety" problems that threaten the existence of the Park.

—answerr to People's Park Questionnaire of the Use Committee

It's now a symbol of the fact that our society does not take care of poor people who are homeless or poor people who have alcohol or other substance abuse problems, so they gather in parks. It bothers me that the University, and society as a whole, think that the way in which you solve homelessness is by moving the homeless people somewhere else.

—Dan Siegel, National Public Radio, Dec. 12, 2006

The very existence of People's Park in such near proximity has been a continual, unwelcome reminder to me of our society's chronic homeless and drug problems. Since I've lived here, I have had to deal with the tension of my more than sufficient life juxtaposed with the more meager lives of those down the street. My response has been to ignore this scene.

When at last I took up an opportunity to distribute bagged lunches to homeless residents in People's Park, my perspective of this place changed completely. I met genuinely nice people, most of a sound mind. I met people who worked hard: collecting cans, tending community gardens. I met people who cared and looked out for others. But unfortunately most of all, I met vulnerable people: people exposed to the elements; exposed to predators and drug pushers; exposed to disease and rot. In most respects, I met people a lot like you and me.

However, the redemptive quality of People's Park is that we see our society for what it is: not without its struggles and flaws. It is better to see the truth, however uneasy to face, than to hide it. If we see our blights in plain sight, and face up to it, we can perhaps tackle a real problem. And if we look a little harder, we can see a whole lot of good things happening in a place where we least expect.

—www.thisplaceis.com

Some of my radical, liberal friends from 15 years back were becoming disgusted with the Park. One of my more noble liberals preferred to work for social justice from his antiseptic non-profit offices, while still taking offense at these people. He now wanted to get those dope smoking bums out. He was once the chic radical fighting the establishment—now, he and his associates are the establishment, only he did not know it…There's freedom here of a kind that most Americans have forgotten. It is a freedom akin to crossing the Frontier in a covered wagon. "Home, home on the range." It is dangerous, lonely, and often alienating. But space and time are your own in a fundamental sense that no mortgage payer or common renter now know.

—Americ Azevedo, www.well.com

Food and clothing are human rights! Every park in the world should dispense food and clothing. Free Speech is a civil right. People's Park is known world wide for Free Speech. Stand up for human and civil rights! Stand up for People's Park! U.C. Out of the Park! Democratize the Regents!

—David Nadel

There's always been lots of drug dealing "within a block of People's Park", even before it was a park. Telegraph Avenue has long been a major regional market in the illicit herb and other contraband commodities. Although such trading may be essentially victimless, People's Park Council has always held (with university agreement) that commercial activity of any kind is wholly alien to the spirit and purpose of the park. Business should be transacted elsewhere, if at all.

—David Axelrod, *Daily Cal* Dec. 1, 1987

"If people were dealing drugs on Sproul Plaza they wouldn't put a dormitory there to stop it".

—Clifford Fred, *Oakland Tribune*, April 21, 1988

Some people who feel that when African Americans just hang out then that's drug dealing. Well it isn't, okay.

—Jim Channin, interview Oct 2006

People's Park
We will defend this place
to the last drop of beer
and the first drop of rain.

—Julia Vinograd, 1984

People's Park is a place where you can get grass or sit on the grass. It is a beautiful place and we should keep it that way.

—Moby Theobald

Enjoy a visit to People's Park
I was in People's Park Monday, it was a beautiful day, and it was beautiful in the park. The sun was shining. Then I went to a bulletin board in the park. There was an article posted. It was written about the park and at the end was a statement by some ASUC senator named Kevin Sabet. He said the park was a "supermarket for drugs." What a crock....

People who don't understand should just go to the park, and enjoy it. Then they would see through the propaganda. It really is nice to have a place to go and get away a little bit from the cars and trucks, buses, pollution, noise, blasting "music"...and get some peace... in People's Park.

—John J. Delmos, letter *Berkeley Daily Planet* April 11, 2000

...Anybody interested in learning about People's Park might want to spend a few minutes talking with neighbors who live near the park. I have spoken with a number of these people, and most of them can provide personal accounts of observing the drug dealing, drinking violent altercations, and other problems that occur frequently in the park. Also, they can tell you about the theft, littering, used needles, trespassing, vandalism, urination and defecation which they deal with at their residences. The perception that People's Park is a dangerous place is not based upon imagination.

—Emily Pearce, response to Delmos letter April 13, 2000

—Sparky, courtesy B.N. Duncana

Today, that land is more than a symbol of free speech. It is more than a remembrance of government folly and principled citizen response. It is the actual fact of authority having lost its authority. It is, and it should continue to be, a living reminder to our leaders that they govern by the consent of the governed and when they betray that trust we, not they, shall have the final word.

—Jon Read, "Keeping a short leash"
Berkeley Voice **Sept. 5, 1991**

What People's Park was, was civil disobedience, but I would reframe it, say it was "civil initiative". When government or authority does something that is so outrageously stupid, like tear down these blocks..., you get a spontaneous response, that's civil initiative. We don't see enough of that now.

— Sim Van der Ryn, interview Nov. 8, 2007

Blows to People's Park are blows to some people of valuable spirit and inspiration who often could be called "a down-under fringe of society" or "alternative-mode", who belong to a special Berkeley trend I call "off-beat and proud". As one of these people, I feel that if powers that be can eliminate People's Park, by the same token I myself can be eliminated.

—B. N. Duncan, June 8, 1994

This is how America works. People's Park is small: for a lot of us, it hit the heart of something much larger...The American system is the system that allows corporations to rake it in while workers must struggle to keep alive. The American system cannot solve its own problems because it is the system that causes those problems. Capitalism is DESIGNED to benefit only a few, at the expense of the many. **—OutCry, 1969**

—*Noah Berger Daily Cal Nov. 30, 1995*

They established a reputation for progressive activism that Berkeley holds to this day. But more than that, they affected the history of the world by affirming the people's right and ability to challenge established authority and to attempt to seize control of intolerable situations.

—Stephanie Manning, "15th Anniversary of PP",
Berkeley Voice, **May 16, 1984**

Many of us originally saw the homeless as undesirables but now realize that "there but for the grace of a few mortgage payments" goes the entire middle class...This is why having the homeless visible in the park is really a free speech issue. The right of the homeless to be visible, smack dab in the center of cities, is fundamental to our government. And defending that right is an act of principled citizenship.
—Jon Read, "An appeal to new UC students about People's Park", *Daily Cal,* **Oct. 8, 1991**

Ecology Center Recycling Dance

The semantics of the debate on People's Park are carefully couched in politically correct wording, seldom using words like "class", "race", or "gentrification". Instead it is worded as issues of "comfort" and "safety". What's really going down is that the Park has become a sanctuary for people who are increasingly marginalized. Skyrocketing rents, closed psychiatric wards and spinning times have left many homeless and unwelcome in other parts of the city. It's challenging all right. In the face of all this, the Park has provided a remarkable service—giving tangible, physical support and more subtly providing a scattered, yet real web of community for those most in need. Unfortunately this creates a place that is understandably "uncomfortable" to those who are used to more predictable and controlled environments.

—Sonnie Day, *Slingshot*, Jan. 24, 2008

The real questions, as most people understood them turned on matters of private property. Park People were charged with trespassing on private land and with refusing to avail themselves of the established procedures...First, it is important to point out that it was not the "radicals" who destroyed "private" property..."private" property had already been pre-empted the previous year when the University obtained control over, and then destroyed, the private residences...In fact, the University and other big businesses like it are obtaining greater and greater control over our economy, our means of transportation, over our health care, urban development, and—as in Berkeley, even over our means of leisure. These big corporations continue to invoke the language of private rights. But they invoke it to hide the fact that they control large-scale social resources in their own interests.

— "People's Park Crisis Chronology" Armed Profits Affinity Group For the Radical Student Union and the Park Negotiating Committee July 29, 1969

For anybody who might hear this who hasn't been to the park, just go to the park, sit there, sit there for an hour and watch and sit and be with it and you'll see yeah, there are people who have some problems, and what one of us can say we don't have problems?...A little more compassion might be in order. And that's part of why I do spend time with my kids in the park, besides that it's beautiful. I believe as a parent, it is absolutely my responsibility that my kids not develop ideas based on other peoples' biases. They need to experience, and if they have concerns about something we'll talk about them and invariably my kids end up getting the injustice of what's going on. By being in the Park, and by talking with people who are probably homeless...lo and behold they recognize that we are all human.

—Maxina Ventura People's Park Community Advisory Board meeting Nov. 5, 2007, recorded by Robert Eggplant

In People's Park, the Berkeley community tried to build something of its own. It wasn't much to begin with, but it was something new, to replace the existing "order." Just as in Vietnam, just as in Detroit, in Watts, everywhere, this attempt was met with the most vicious suppression. The struggle for self-determination everywhere is the struggle for the new society. Bullets, clubs and tear-gas cannot and will not end it.
—*OutCry*, 1969

A cop drove his car into the Park and we all said "No cop cars in the Park!!" Food Not Bombs was serving and there was a ton of people there. The cop responded that "He would park where ever the hell he wanted, By Gosh" He went on around the Park I.D.ing folks and we resumed eating. Being served was a potato/peas/spinach concoction that was not going over very well and I took my plate and set it on the police car. Everyone else started to do the same. And then it happened. The thing that made me a true believer and servant to the people till this very day. At least 100 pigeons, maybe more, descended upon the police car and started eating that gluey concoction as only pigeons can do and in no time at all they had completely slathered the police car in about an inch of FNB cement. When people started to notice, the laughter got louder and louder. The cop caught on and started running down from the top of the Park. His keys and flashlight and what-all a jangling, he screamed, "Who did this to my car!!!" And I yelled "Arrest the pigeons!!"... I know that

the current pigeons are the grandchildren of the glorious birds of that day and I always feed them, salute them, and if I see someone abusing them I tell them the story and they are looked upon with a new respect and the stature of true People's Park Warriors.

—Danny McMullan, March 2009

—Roosey Stephens

"The issues surrounding the defense of People's Park are all wrapped up around each other like the layers of an onion. — **C. beck , "Save People's Park: A work in progress" 1992**

One of the things that is always left out of the story, which is a lot of the Park, is that before the anti-war movement, the area where the park is, in fact anything past Grove Street, no black people, no black kids could venture past that until the anti-war movement and now with the sort of rest area of the park and now they're allowed to hang in the park. I remember having my friend over and he says, 'Hey you know Mike, we couldn't come over here before the sixties the cops would, you know, beat us up or we would get arrested.' So that's not anything that's printed.
—Michael Delacour, interview Jan. 17, 2007

The University may technically hold legal title to the land, but People's Park itself belongs to the People of Berkeley, not the university. The community created it, maintained it, defended it, and paid for it with the blood of James Rector, the blinding of a local artist, and injuries to hundreds of others. Despite the violent seizure of the Park the community never considered the University's occupation of the land legitimate. **—Elliot Cohen, "UC students should vote to support People's Park" Berkeley Daily Planet April 12, 2000**

The organic movement, much like environmentalism and feminism, has deep roots in the sixties' radicalism that briefly flourished on this site; organic is one of several tributaries of the counterculture that ended up disappearing into the American mainstream, but not before significantly altering its course. And if you trace that particular tributary all the way back to its spring, your journey will eventually pass through this park.
—Michael Pollan, *Omnivore's Dilemma*, 2006

But the Park remains; people still live there. For nearly 40 years People's Park has been a symbol and a home to people who did not or could not live the "American dream"—all for different reasons. ...I've had my moments close to the edge. Only my friends kept me from the street. My business partner had similar troubles. You owe it to yourself to hang out with the dispossessed. As the Depression proved, very little separates us from the street.
—Americ Azevedo, "At home in the Park", philosopher-at-large.blogspot.com

People's Park is not an island. It cannot be separated from the child poverty and the poverty of Richmond and in Oakland and in West Berkeley. Every time you read about a university spokesman saying that People's Park is not safe I'm going to tell you that none of us are safe until all boats rise...The park to me represents the quality of mercy," it's not strained, it dropeth like the gentle rain". That's what it means to me. We must never forget that 40 years ago, only Frankie, the woman from England, the heroin addict, she was the only homeless person at the time. **—Wendy Schlesinger, 40th Anniversary Founders Forum, April 24, 2009**

COPWATCH

Copwatch was started in March of 1990 in response to escalating abuse of people in the Telegraph Avenue area of Berkeley...The People's Café, which existed to give support to homeless people in People's Park was taken by the University in the middle of the night. Harassment of homeless people and others was increasing in frequency and severity. People came together out of a mutual understanding that this violence, which targeted the poor, street people, people of color, activists and counter culture types was a direct result of pressure from the University... In 1991 Copwatch worked extensively to document police brutality during the People's Park riots. We documented the introduction of rubber and wooden bullets into the Berkeley police arsenal. We also held demonstrations against the brutal beating of a Berkeley Police Review Commissioner named Osha Neumann.

—www.highvibrations.org

Since the People's Park riots of 1991, Copwatch has had its hands full. Copwatch type groups have sprung up all over the country and, over the past 20 years, copwatching has become a widely recognized form of community based police accountability. Although Copwatch has grown as a consciousness over the past 20 years, it still reflects the values of the park that helped to create it. Focus on and respect for the rights of the poorest and most marginalized people is a core value of the park culture and Copwatch has People's Park to thank for refreshing and perhaps instilling that principle in this generation of activists.

—Andrea Pritchett, June 28, 2009

—*jwoodard.best.vwh.net*

—*www.berkeleycopwatch.org*

Bad Cop, No Donut

Since the riots, Berkeley's police watchdog group, Copwatch, has had its hands full. Copwatch activist Andrea Pritchett sees the People's Park riots as the climax of a pattern of police harassment which had been underway for several years. She says that Copwatch exists to "observe police as they interact with members of the community. We attempt to photograph and videotape police actions. We also educate people about their rights, especially their right to observe. And we educate the public that this is not just random incidents—its a systematic campaign to relocate the homeless people and counterculture people from Berkeley."

—Bill Weinberg, "Berkeley's People's Park: Counterculture landmark is once again Battleground" *Downtown* **(NYC paper) Oct. 1991**

BERKELEY FREE CLINIC

The Free Clinic was really begun by a group of medics who had been responding to injuries from the violence that the state brought against people who were building the park, in opposition to the war. Once the heat, the flames of that initial struggle were settling a little bit, I think people were reminded that this is really important, this community we built. How do we take responsibility ...provide health care? With that focus people came together to do it in a different way and started this community health project, the Berkeley Free Clinic. They continue to this very day...and onto tomorrow.

— Jon L, interview Mar. 5, 2009

The Free Clinic was founded in 1969 as a "street medicine" clinic that quickly found a niche and a permanent home in the Berkeley community. It has become an icon in the area, and has served countless thousands in a variety of ways during its 35-year history...The Berkeley Free Clinic is a volunteer—based, non-profit organization, which has been providing much-needed medical, dental, counseling, HIV testing, and other services since 1969. The Berkeley Community Health Project, Inc., as it is legally known, has also been a major force in health education, running extensive training programs for volunteers and others in the community.

—www.berkeleyfree clinic.org

HEALTH CARE FOR PEOPLE NOT PROFIT

Stolen Lives Project, names of those killed by police

Fourth of July TV Smash

Earth Goddess Puppet

Fourth of July Flag Burning

Jon. L sharing food

107

Michael Delacour   —Harold Adler

Free Speech has always been an important part of People's Park. It was born from the political and cultural milieu of the Free Speech Movement on the Berkeley campus five years earlier. Michael Delacour, "father" of the Park, was motivated to clean up the lot specifically to have a place to gather to have concerts and political rallies.

Max Scheer, editor of the Berkeley Barb
—Harold Adler

—courtesy Max Ventura

—Greg Jalbert

—Zachary Ogen

—courtesy Lisa Stephens

Utah Phillips
—Charles Gary

—courtesy Christopher McKinney

PEOPLE'S PARK
FREE RADIO
87.9 FM
APR 25
TURN ON · TUNE IN · TAKE OVER!
LET 10,000 TRANSMITTERS BLOOM!

—Zachary Ogen

—Lydia Gans

—Zachary Ogen

David Nadel set up a table and signs every weekend for months before and after the volleyball courts were installed. He also published and posted the monthly "UC Scandal Sheet".

—Zachary Ogen

THE DAILY CALI

VOLUME CXXI, NO. 118   WEDNESDAY, AUGUST 12,

UC regents settle rights suit

Chalk sloganeers get $25,000 for People's Park arrest

Christopher McKinney and David Kamola arrested for "petty vandalism" for writing political slogans with chalk on the sidewalk by People's Park by UC police who detain them for 7 hours. The two file suit in US District Court within two weeks and win the suit a year later, netting $25,000.
—from Bob Sparks Chronology

There's a kind of spark of rebelliousness, humanity that is expressed. Even though it is not an example for our youth, it is people acting out their unique impulses, their free spirits.
—Jane Scheer, interview, Nov. 1, 2007

—Lydia Gans

—C. beck

The meeting started at 7:30pm in the Pauley Ballroom on campus. By 8pm it was packed with hundreds of pissed-off park supporters, waiting to denounce the university administration, the UCB police and the down-town Telegraph Ave Merchants Assoc.—all on an open mike... It was a hellish marathon—young anarchists shouting, aging park activists weeping in anger and banging on bongos, various street people reciting poetry—The line to speak snaked through the ballroom and then looped around the room's inside perimeter...130 speakers later, (I am not kidding) the meeting finally ended after midnight, but not before a mini demonstration erupted. It seems an additional 200 speakers who were on the speaking waiting list weren't going to just pack up their bongos and go home.

These are hardcores—the group of people who demonstrate against the people's park demonstrators. A verbal fight ensued as those who were being cutoff attacked those who already spoke.

—May 18, 1994
A collection of opinions collected by Tom Leonard for the City of Berkeley /University of California, People's Park 1993-94 Annual Evaluation

X-Plicit Players   —Charles Gary

The defense of the stage and the Free Box are in fact quite important and indicate why People's Park is such an important space in the current history of American public space. The stage was built explicitly as a space for free speech and political action, and it has remained a key center for rallies and organizing efforts in the city. In this sense, People's Park was constructed as a public space for politics, as a place where political involvement and debate were encouraged and in a way that stood at odds with (but not disconnected from) the more orderly politics of the traditional parties, elections, council meetings, and the like .

—Don Mitchell
"The Right to the City: Social Justice and the Fight for Public Space", Guilford Press 2003

UC Berkeley has lost its battle against amplified sound in People's Park. Declaring any ban on amplified sound "an unconstitutional violation of...First Amendment rights to speak and assemble", Alameda County Court Judge John Sutter issued a permanent restraining order Friday stopping the university from enforcing a ban on amplified sound in the park.
— Steve Ipson *Daily Cal* **Dec. 7, 1987**

Funky Nixons

—*Lydia Gans*

A big part of free speech is being able to use it. For those who don't own TV stations, bulletin boards and places to publicly pronounce beliefs are essential to sharing our ideas. The struggle for these outlets has been played out with persistence as the University has destroyed bulletin boards, kiosks, and paints over slogans on the Free Speech Stage.

CELEBRATIONS

The Park is the physical place that we gather in time, to celebrate, to share culture, to protest, and express the desires and creativity of our communities. There have been countless amazing coming togethers in People's Park. There are events that happen year after year and events that happen once. Anyone can organize an event to be held freely in the Park. The Park was born of a desire to have a place for rallies and concerts, and having a gathering place is still of utmost importance for a healthy connected community. If there is an emergency we will go to the park. We hold memorials there. And especially we celebrate. Every anniversary of the Park itself, and many other times. The right to hold amplified events was re-established in a legal ruling in 1987. To me, nothing seems more sacred and beneficial for the Park than when "I Dance Upon Her Sacred Ground to the Music in the Air".

May it continue.

—Jane Scheer **115**

Wavy Gravy — *Michael Kinney*

—*Zachary Ogen*

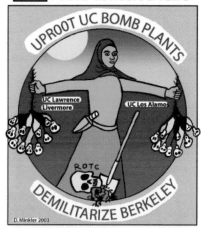

Fourteenth Anniversary 1983

—David Axelrod

Country Joe McDonald

—Zachary Ogen

117

—John Spicer

—Zachary Ogen

Anyhow, big ol' party one block from my apartment. Craziness spilling over everywhere —public nakedness, a band, ninjas, rides, bicycle rodeos (don't ask me), a crazy bus, PortoSan's, a band, and more!

**—www.hodgeslab.org/2004/04/peoples_park_
anniversary.html**

2morrow there is a sk8 party in peoples park with a whole slew o' ramps and lots of athletes busting out fearless tricks! sunday 27 from 1-6! wish the sick were playing. usually they have some hippie nonsense bands with nudy berkeley locals who impose their visual violations on us all. but overall its just nice 2 see good skateboarding all day. bad religion is performing @ 230 ha ha psyched you all out! skateboarding is not a crime. ciao.

—4eyes www.thesick.com

I went to the People's Park festival just after noon, the "thirty-third anniversary of People's Park festival" to be exact...There were folks from the old days, grey hair, still fighting wars long lost. The same sweet smell of marijuana, the same drums and chants, the same dancing shadows holding hands in the crowd. And the others, the younger ones: leather, metal studs, skate boards, purple hair, sleeping bags, anger and madness, attracted to a celebration of a time when the street met the man and the street won. Either that or the free music and the one or two naked women.

**—The Sole Proprietor's Journal
www.apersonalsite.com, April 28th, 2002**

Anniversary Party at People's Park
by Julia Vinograd

Drummers on stage, circles of people whirling,
rags and feathers.
We're a tribe, we're on the cover
of National Geographic where native women
carry baskets on their heads, bare breasts swaying.
We don't have any baskets,
we've got some basket cases
and a few girls shrug their shirts off
while freckles pour down from the sky.
A bottle of red wine goes around a circle
of reddening faces, brighter than blood.
Broken teeth grin. Beer cans blossom.
Enough spills for our thirsty ghosts.
Lovers' hands get big and blurry.
We're a tribe, we move in mystic circles,
like the drunk said when the cop
told him to walk a straight line.
Damp grass licks our bare feet like a puppy's tongue.
Half the people here can't do anything
but magic
and magic dissolves in the rain.
It rained yesterday, it will rain tomorrow
but today we're having a party
in the hole of a hostile donut.
The thing about the park is
you can't just go there
unless the park comes out to meet you.
Today it has. We're a tribe.
In spite of a sound system
from hell
we're using the music to
climb ourselves
like dancing up a rusty fire
escape
to steal the fire.
**— October 2005
Street Spirit**

—Zachary Ogen

Julia Vinograd

YOU ARE INVITED TO ATTEND
THE 40TH ANNIVERSARY OF
PEOPLE'S PARK
1969
AN AFTERNOON OF
MUSIC, MEMORIES & MAGIC
SUNDAY, APRIL 26 NOON-SIX
IS (from Berkeley High) ✹ JERRY GARTHWAITE & FAMILY
Shelley Doty ✹ COUNTRY JOE McDONALD
JONATHAN RICHMAN ✹ CAROL DENNEY
ALL NATIONS SINGERS ✹ PHOENIX
MOROR ZEN BELLY DANCE ✹ FOOD NOT BOMBS
WWW.PEOPLESPARK.ORG   (510)390-0830

THE 40TH ANNIVERSARY of
PEOPLE'S PARK
WEEK of EVENTS
Sat 4/18 ACOUSTIC MUSIC & ACTION DAY People's Park noon-dark

Mon 4/20 PEOPLE'S PARK FILM FEST 7pm, 2951 Derby, Berkeley

Tues 4/21 GOT FREE SPEECH? FORUM 6-7:30pm, Berkeley Public Library then the PEOPLE'S PARK POTLUCK & FOLK SHOW 8-11pm UU Fellowship, 1924 Cedar, Berkeley

Wed 4/22 HEALTH FAIR 2-5pm in People's Park sponsored by Easy Does It

Thurs 4/23 PEOPLE'S POETRY 7-10pm Caffe Med 2475 Telegraph

Fri 4/24 FOUNDERS FORUM Founders, Poets & Music 4:30pm-late. $15 ish Ashkenaz 1317 San Pablo Ave, Berk.

Sun 4/26 PEOPLE'S PARK 40TH ANNIVERSARY CONCERT 12-6pm in People's Park. Food, Fun. www.peoplespark.org

1969 PEOPLE'S PARK 40TH ANNIVERSARY 2009

SEEN CONCERTS

Tyrone Ingram

The SEEN Festival 2006 - 11th Annual World Reggae Soul Festival

On Saturday afternoon August 16th (2003), many in Berkeley California's historic People's Park witnessed what was for a certainty a day of much-needed reggae bubblin, roots and culture. Once again reggae festival promoter S. Tyrone Ingram of the Oakland based entertainment company; Fox Ingram Enterprise, staged again the ever-growing SEEN Festival that after this exciting show, is now heading into it 9th consecutive and successful year...One of the more major and popular events held there (in the park) over the past years has been The SEEN Festival; an annual free reggae worldbeat benefit music festival aiding battered women and homeless & displaced families that has been, according to the locals "going strong" since 1997.

—maxpages.com/seen2000

121

BERKELEY MARDI GRAS

The One True Church of the Great Green Frog celebrates Mardi Gras in Berkeley with an all day parade that comes by the Park for dancing, relaxing and dining on Food Not Bombs. Laissez Les Bon Temps Rouler.

—Crow

—Crow

—Crow

—Crow

—Crow

—Marion "Moe" Shelby

—Crow

—Crow

—Crow

Pagan Festival

—Venee Cal-Ferrer

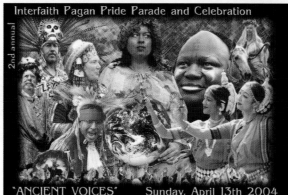

Interfaith Pagan Pride Parade and Celebration

2nd annual

"ANCIENT VOICES" Sunday, April 13th 2004

—www.thepaganalliance.org

—Venee Cal-Ferrer (both)

ISHTAR EGG HUNT in PEOPLE'S PARK

ALL CHILDREN WELCOME

SUNDAY APRIL 11th

Krishna Concert

Hare Krishna Hare Krishna Krishna Kris

124

— *Katherine Brewer*

— *Katherine Brewer*

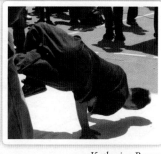

— *Katherine Brewer*

headliners: Lyrics Born, Medusa, Crown City Rockers
featuring: Freelancers Utd.

I do not frequent this park, but I have had a chance to go to at least 3 annual "Hip Hop in the Park" events here for free...Free music, b-boy/b-girl exhibitions, and live graffiti. Always happens in May, and at least a handful of the artists are worth checking out. Usually, one big name and the rest are local artists that are trying to make a name for themselves. If you are about supporting underground and up and coming artists, this should be your stomping grounds. Did I say this was FREEEEEEE?!

Anna L. April 20, 2008 Yelp

125

Rep. Barbara Lee

Zachary RunningWolf

— *Roosevelt Stephens*

Funky Nixons

Marsha Feinland

Michael Delacour and Paul Sawyer   —*Danny McMullen*

Gerald Smith

Cynthia Johnson

127

Residence HALL ASSEMBLY @ uc berkeley

For more info on RHA: http://reshall.berkeley.edu/rha

Events
• 12:45 ~ TUG-OF-WAR
• 1:25 ~ 3-LEGGED RACE
• 2:20 ~ PIE-EATING CONTE
• 3:00 ~ Water Balloon Tos

Bearfest
2007

DO IT YOURSELF FEST

D.I.Y
FFS

what the
hell is going
on here!

12:30 bike across the u.s.
        massage trade
1:30   gay shame ♥'s you)
        bicycle repair
2:00   knot tying PLANT
                   WALK
2:30   instrument making
        jujitsu
3:30   BOOK BINDING
        WORM bin construction
4:30   poi (fire dancing)
→ all day AT MIKE'S TABLE
  · street pharmacology · alcohol
  · alternative toothpaste · vegan
  · mushrooms on a log · bird

the BARRINGTON COLLECTIVE
Infocenter

home crafts

PIRATE
RADIO

ONE LOVE FESTIVAL

Phoenix & AfterBuffalo
The Journey Continues

129

Heavy Schtetl   —Elisa Smith

Fifteen plays   —courtesy Arthur Fonseca

Patriot Rally

—David Blackman

My fondest memory of people's park was last year, when they had their anniversary celebration. We were sitting in the sun, listening to some bad folk singer, when a group of twenty people, naked and covered with mud from head to toe, ran through chanting, singing and beating drums. I don't know if it was a protest or a tribal gathering, but I thought, "This is what this park is for!"
— "A collection of opinions collected by Tom Leonard for the City of Berkeley /UC", May 18, 1994

—David Blackman

Funky Nixons

Shortly after the Iraq war started we heard of a "Patriot Rally" to be held in People's Park. Oh the nerve! And yet we were all about free speech. So we showed up dressed as sheep and carrying signs, only to have been fooled by the most outrageous presentation of a peeing Elvis, the gay choir all in satin red, white and blues, and the Extra Action Marching band (seen above). SF pranksters were keeping the park polished. —ed.

The Really Really Free Market

Cinnamon and Gypsy's wedding
—courtesy B.N. Duncan

The People's Park Players

—John Jekabson

The spring began with a couple concerts that came off quite well. Robert Hunter of the Grateful Dead played a May gig there, as did a band formed by a couple former members of Creedence Clearwater Revival. Despite some rather disconcerting public sex in one corner of the park, things went smoothly. Not Disney World, but not bad for a bunch of freaks. **—Ron Jacobs, "Long Live People's Park!",** *Counter Punch,* **May 23, 2003**

—courtesy Debbie Moore

COMMUNITY

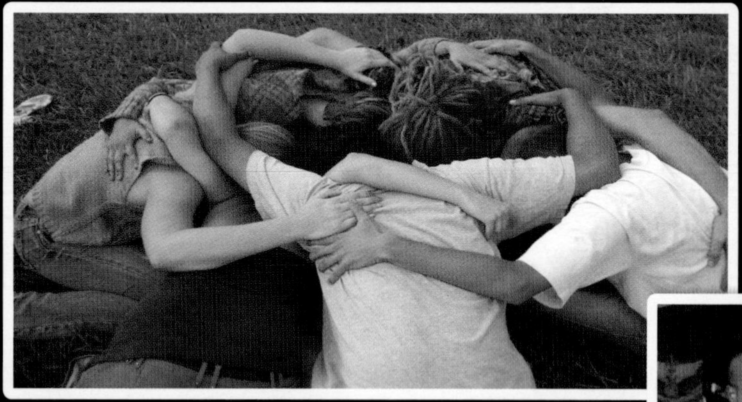

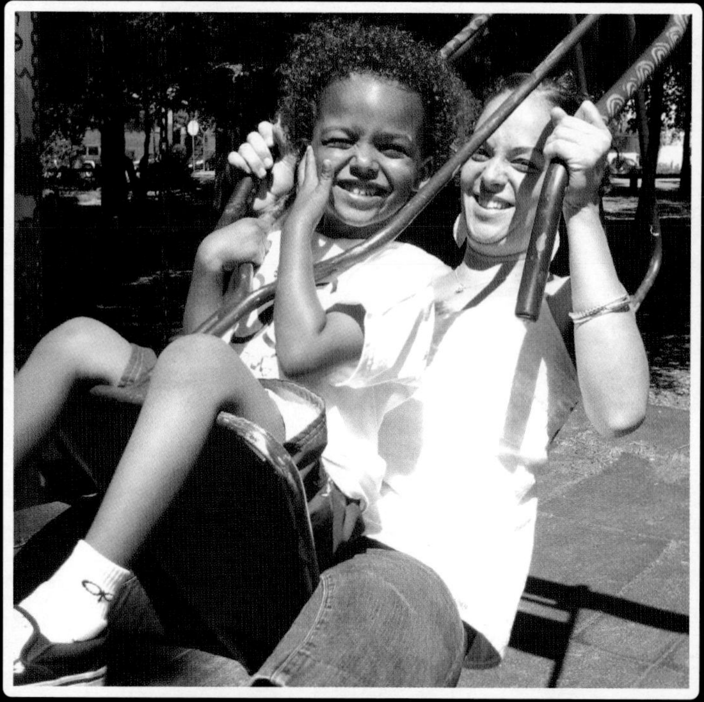

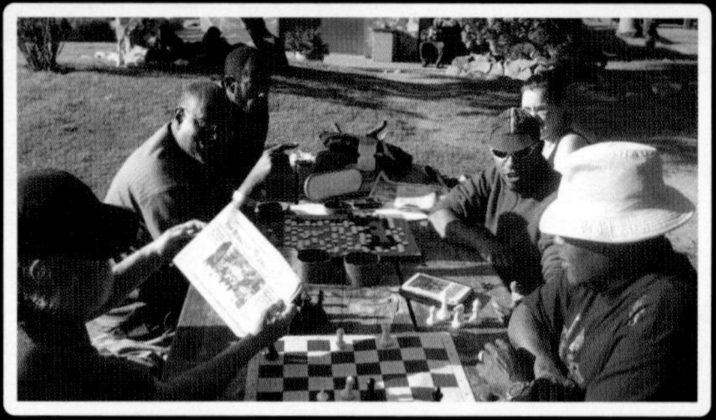

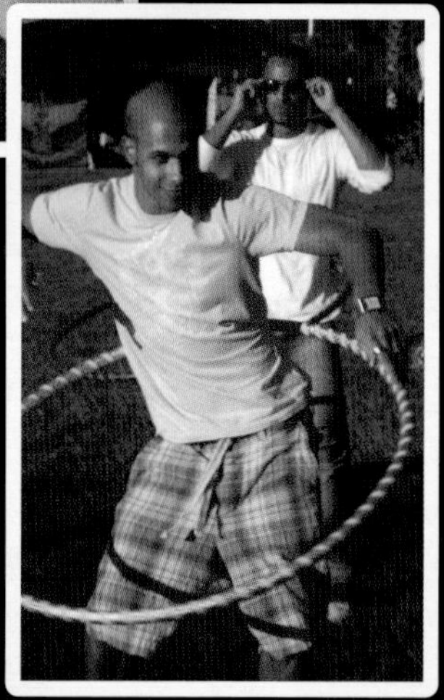

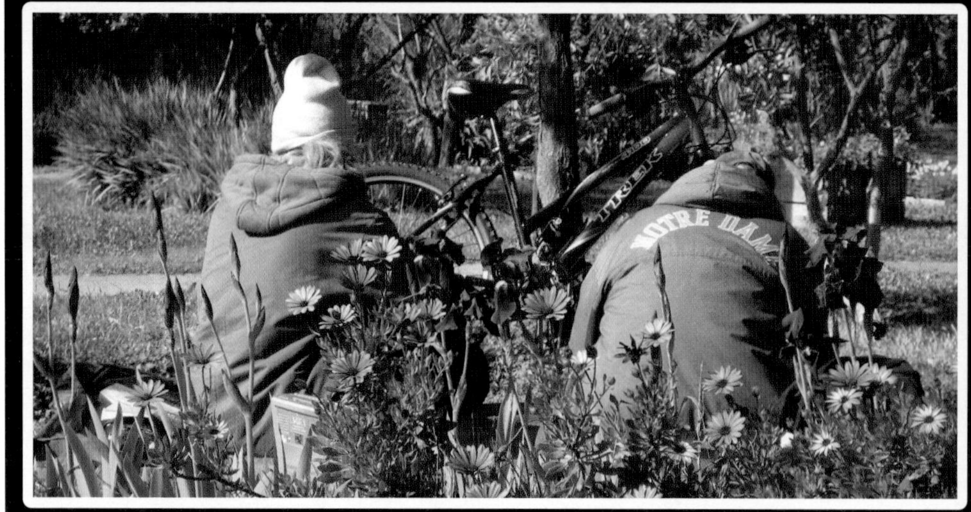

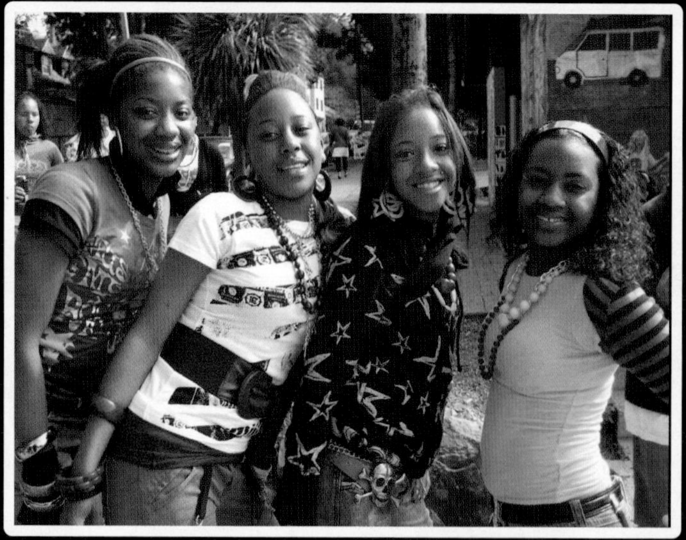

—courtesy David Axelrod

—Gary Freedman "Berkeley a Self Portrait"

—courtesy David Axelrod

—Jane Scheer

—Jane Scheer

—*Lydia Gans*

—*Lydia Gans*

People Park has for over 25 years held archetypal significance as a national symbol for how our urban culture deals with the homeless. ..For everyone involved People's Park has become both a collective 'hot spot' and a 'sacred place': a territorial intersection of competing interests and perspectives, and a symbolic altar on which widely different perspectives, are played out in human minds and bodies.

The Berkeley Religious Coalition with the Homeless is working with nearby churches and religious organizations in organizing a weekend workshop sponsored by C.G. Jung Institute analysts Arthur Colman, MD and Pilar Montero, Ph.d and analysts from the Awakening Collective Consciousness group with the goal of releasing some of the archetypal 'heat' surrounding People's Park and helping to create greater understanding among all parties of the symbolic role the park plays- and why this must be respected. Sub-goals of the workshop are: 1) learning about scapegoating; 2) examining experiences of victims and victimizers; 3) seeing the ways groups are economically and socially vulnerable; 4) better understanding humanity as one community.

—Awakening the Unconscious at People's Park Weekend Workshop June 1-2 1996, Berkeley Religious Coalition with the Homeless (flier)

PEOPLE'S PARK

YOUR HELP & SUPPORT IS NEEDED

What You Can Do

- Nightly Vigils- Come to the Park between 9 PM & 10 PM and stay as long as possible. Bring candles and drums. Meet on Dwight Way across from People's Park if the

People's Park is a legacy that has been bequeathed upon you. It has been given to us by two generations of activists rioting, sweating, and negotiating. These activists invest themselves in the community and the environment rather than in the economy.

—Arthur Fonseca "What is People's Park?"

135

He was one of eight Jungian analysts who had been invited by the Berkeley Ecumenical Chaplaincy to the Homeless and the Berkeley Religious Coalition with the Homeless to lead a two-day workshop that would... explore "the symbolic/archetypal level on which People's Park operates in our psyches."...

Then Charles Townes, Frances Townes' husband and a recipient of a Nobel Prize for his invention of the laser, stood up and plunged his hands into the pockets of his gray flannel trousers. "I've always liked parks," he said, his voice puzzled. "What's wrong with a park? I think we should have more of them. The problem isn't the park, it's how we treat each other."...

"Just having a place where I can go and find people like myself. It's like a haven, a home away from home." said Yukon Hannibal.

—Dashka Slater "Children of Paradise"
EastBay Express, **July 12, 1996**

Thunder and I had organized a prayer circle in People's Park and Fran Macy and Joanna Macy and some of the homeless people and other members of the Berkeley community stood with us in a circle and we were offering our prayers and meditations for peace and a flock of birds flew over us. It was a prayer on the wing of the birds. It was an "Aha" moment moving beyond what separates us.

—Redwood Mary, interview Mar. 14, 2009

Men of the "cloth", including Rev. Richard York (from the Berkeley Free Church) with flowing robes, blessed People's Park in typical "street" style yesterday, complete with litany, chanting, the ram's horn, candle burning, and thinly veiled inferences of what will happen "when the bulldozers move in." On hand were more than 1,000 persons of varying ages...

—Gazette, May 12, 1969

People's Park Consecrated

Leading off the ceremony yesterday was Father Jim Conway, a Roman Catholic. He was followed by Isaac Bonowitz, who is a convert to the Universal Church of Life...Next was Dick York, minister of the Free Church, who led the crowd in chants of "Power to the People" and "Out, Demons, Out." York, clad in a multicolored African shirt, then pronounced, "In the name of Jesus, decontaminate this place of evil demons and fill the air with vibrations of love." A Krishna fellow draped in salmon colored silks, a whitewash stripe painted down his nose, chanted "Hare Krishna" as he lit offerings of fire and incense "to protect

this land from the University." Then he blew a ferocious blast through a sea shell. A Moslem, clad in conservative suit and tie but wearing a red fez, spoke briefly.

—San Francisco Examiner May 12, 1969

—Elihu Blotnick

137

Even today, when people walk by People's Park their gaze is somewhat affected by the politics of class and race in a diverse nexus of both. To white Americans who are not acquainted with people of color, specifically with African American males, and to those who rarely encounter very low-income or homeless people of all races, the Park can seem to be a dangerous, unusual place-especially at night.

—Wendy Schlesinger
"The Whole World is Watching"

In a recent Orwellian twist, the design architects hired by UC Berkeley published a report declaring that People's Park was under-utilized and lacked diversity. In fact, People's Park has more users per area than probably any other Berkeley park and is arguably one of the more diverse places on Earth. What "lack of diversity" meant in their report was that some well-off, white, "nice" people don't feel comfortable using the Park.

—Sonnie Day Slingshot.tao.ca Jan. 24, 2008

It has been said that the University of California may own the land that contains People's Park but it doesn't own the spirit that is the Park. This little bit of green space in one of the most densely populated sections of the city serves an incredibly diverse population. And it is maintained, nurtured and supported by a diverse set of people, from teens to old folks, gardeners, food providers, churches, political activists and by Berkeley City Councilmember Kriss Worthington.

—Lydia Gans "Rebuilding the Freebox in
People's Park" *Street Spirit* **Dec. 2005**

—courtesy Lisa Stephens

—*Rosevelt Stephens*

Reviews from www.yelp.com

I'm glad People's Park exists. It's good as a shortcut. It has a great history. But honestly, I wouldn't hang out here. The basketball court gets good use. Yes, sometimes there are naked people in the park.
—Rachel R., Santa Clara 03/24/06 Yelp

Welcome to reality and a chance to add your touch. It's unpredictable, magical, historical and YOU can make it better. Just by daring to be "the People" and being there. Play frisbee, picnic, volunteer with one of the many organizations that serve free food, drop off your old clothes, find some new clothes (the University keeps tearing down the "Freebox" but you can still find some interesting stuff in the pile in the driveway)....Sure it's got a bad rap and it is a refuge for all those folks that would get kicked off campus but the times I've visited I had some really interesting conversations and a good time. Don't believe the hype. Check it out for yourself. Watch "Berkeley in the 60's" and you might really appreciate this Park's link with our past.

—Cyndi J., Berkeley 8/29/2006 Yelp

Nudity doesn't bother me. What bothers me so much about People's Park, is that it is owned by the University of California, and they are too PC to do anything about it. During the housing crunch and meetings with the building planners resulted in them telling us that the pressure was to (sic) great by activists and the people of Berkeley. Well Berkeley, you don't own the land and quite frankly you're perfectly willing to allow it to fester....I, on the other hand, am a student of the UC and pay taxes and tuition and the UC once needed more housing and some better student facilities. Now we need more space. There are a lack of classrooms and office space for several departments. And still the activists think any suggestion of a compromise is outrageous....University owned, People's park is an irritating, drug infested, smelly door to hell. Students can't go anywhere near it for fear of being robbed, hurt or worse and dammit it should be our park. I want it turned into something nice and not a source of crime in this city. Seriously, map crime in this city on south-side and it pretty much centers on people's park and radiates outward. If it does have historical value, that's what a plaque is for....And if you say, where will all the people go? That's what home and housing services are for. I'm sorry but a crime cesspool does not commemorate the wonderful activism that happened 20 years ago. It just doesn't.   **—Katharine C., Berkeley 08/16/2006 Yelp**

crazy, naked people that will run after you for a quarter...+2 stars for getting a good workout....-3 stars for being chased.
—Sam Y., Berkeley 04/16/2006 Yelp

The name is essentially a brand with followers and haters, the prior usually citing its' history and the latter citing its' modern symbol of grime and transience...My personal opinion is that this park is great! It houses countless events of significant cultural and social purpose, serving the greater East-bay community, and I believe the University should embrace and promote its' weaving into Cal life a little better. Likewise, I believe the community should step outside their boxes to spruce the place up and make the environment more hospitable to students transitioning from their previous communities to Berkeley.   **—Andrew C., San Francisco 08/18/2008 Yelp**

I guess this park never came out as intended but it's turned into a really "interesting" place regardless.
kim n., Mountain View 09/03/2008 Yelp

A DAY WITHOUT A BUZZ, IS A DAY THAT NEVER WAS!!!

—courtesy Lisa Stephens

—Jane Scheer

I became fascinated that People's Park had every kind of person imaginable…It was never boring, the total opposite of a gated community. To me it was thrilling. It was like going to a movie, or going to a play or reading a book. It wasn't predictable.

—Claire Burch, interview Feb. 28, 2007

The contrast is stunning: chipper, fast-paced, self con-scious white college kids hurry from place to place on the outskirts while all ages and races of bums wander, sit, smoke, read, and sleep in the park. After the dust settled I wasn't sure which group had it figured out better.

—Joe, "my experiences working at St. Vincent de Paul" Oct. 24, 2005

As I interacted with the 100 or so people who walked past my bucket of fruit salad, I realized that there wasn't much to be afraid of. The people in People's Park are just like the rest of us. They're human too.

School is supposed to be a place where you experi-ence new things and change your outlook on life. This assignment helped me see something that I'd glanced at from a distance for three years. People's Park is a different place when viewed from the inside out.

—Tamara Keith, *Daily Cal*

In the Spring of 1990 my business partner and myself stopped at People's Park in Berkeley, California. We sat on a log among the homeless people. Some were cooking their food. Others rolling around in the grass with their loved ones. Some smoked weed and drank booze. They dressed in rags, tie-dye shirts, jeans, long hair, short hair, leather jackets, and bare chests.

And, we, two businessmen, would-be land developers and housing manufacturers where sitting there. Such was the power of People's Park to attract all kinds of folks. A long-time looking patron of the Park came up to us and said, "What are you guys doing here? You don't belong here!"

My partner responded, "We're people too!" We kept sitting. The obviously long- term Park resident, shrugged his shoulders and indicated that we were "okay". Thus, we had established our "turf" on a log. Land title had its own rules here.

—Americ Azevedo, www.well.com

Today I'm going to walk through the park, no matter what they say - and then tonight when I get back to the dorms, I'll tell everyone about it and they'll think I'm either too cool or too silly or something else.

—Dan Lai, members.cox.net

— *Rosevelt Stephens*

141

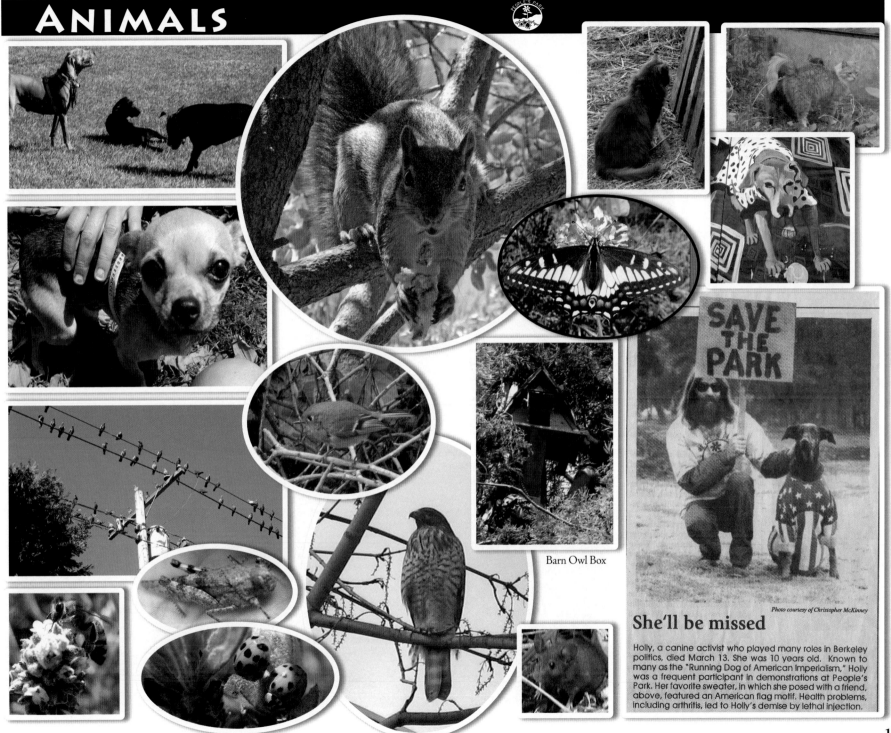

Barn Owl Box

Photo courtesy of Christopher McKinney

She'll be missed

Holly, a canine activist who played many roles in Berkeley politics, died March 13. She was 10 years old. Known to many as the "Running Dog of American Imperialism," Holly was a frequent participant in demonstrations at People's Park. Her favorite sweater, in which she posed with a friend, above, featured an American flag motif. Health problems, including arthritis, led to Holly's demise by lethal injection.

—Jonathan Taylor

— *Rosevelt Stephens*

"People's Park is pretty good as far as competition," said Vishu Shuhakar, a UC Berkeley senior. "But sometimes it's overcrowded and hard to get a pick-up game because there's so many people there." Unique to the park is the number of spectators that gather for a glimpse of the fast-paced action.

—"Ballin' in Berkeley"
***Berkeley Daily Planet* July 25, 2002**

A nice place to waste a day away. I love that in the midst of Berkeley, there's a place where I can always get a hoops game going, and as you'd expect in this town, with all characters--Students, Hustlas, Dads & sons, and even the homeless jump in—some of whom are pretty good. Though watch out for the Homeless Kobe—thankfully, he only copies Mr. Bryants' ball-hogging skills, as far as I can tell...

**— Chris R.,
Yelp Review
Mar. 28, 2006**

—*Jonathan Taylor*

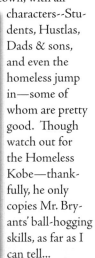

On my recent travels, I came upon a group of chess players while passing People's Park. As I joined the group of kibitzers around one game that had just concluded, the victor looked up at me and asked if I played chess. I said that I did, but hastened to add that I hadn't played tournament chess for many years. Maybe it was that I appeared somewhat older than the other onlookers or perhaps it was my evasive answer, but I could feel his suspicion as he asked me for my rating. When I admitted that I had a master rating, he identified himself as the champion of People's Park.

Having thrown down the gauntlet, he led me to a tabled area near the middle of the park. On this gorgeous day the park overflowed with aging hippies and other park denizens listening to a minor rock concert. It's times like these I'm thankful I'm almost deaf in one ear. Kibitzers and the pungent smell of cannabis started drifting over as he set up his chess equipment. After about half a dozen games and his growing awareness of the real difference in strength between us, we agreed upon one last bout.

— **Kerry Lawless (U.S. Chess Master),**
"Champion of People's Park"
http://www.chessdryad.com Oct. 20, 2002

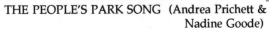

THE PEOPLE'S PARK SONG (Andrea Prichett & Nadine Goode)

Beautiful, beautiful, I'll be bound
By the spirit I see and the love that I've found
Twenty years blood and tears, still here we are
There's no turning back when we've come this far

  It's the park, yeah, People's Park, yeah
  Everybody knows it's a fight for the land
  It's the park, yeah, People's Park, yeah
  Even young and old, they all understand

Miracle, miracle, must be true
Incredible things that the people can do
Everyday, right away, people unite
Lift up our hands to do what is right

Peacefully, happily, for our defense
We feed the people while you build a fence
Anyway, that's ok, try as you will
We tend the land, upon the blood that you spill

(folk verse added by Steve Brady)
Miracle, miracle look what I've found
A big bag of
pot lyin' here
on the ground
Maybe I'll roll
it up, smoke it
with friends
Or sell it to
tourists at ten
bucks a pin.

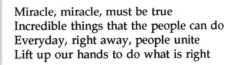

Max Ventura

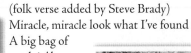

Hali Hammer

149

People's Park remains a land struggle with the University of California. UC holds the paper title to the land and have the legal and police system to back them up. But many believe they abused the use of Eminent Domain and don't rightfully own it. The land was reclaimed and the Park was created by the People. The violence the University used in trying to take it back cemented the People's claim. The University has treated the Park variously over the years. They currently seem to at least understand the desperate need for open space in an area crammed full. The UC personnel hired to interface with the community have not had an easy job.

Donna Spring and Kris Worthington were both active and supportive of the Park during the Volleyball protests and were subsequently elected to the Berkeley City Council where they have been staunch progressive voices.

Until very recently, Peoples Park remained the only development of open space proposed by the University administration that had been stopped. So although many of the more conservative town's people did not participate in the demonstrations, some were glad that people had finally tried to use civil disobedience in protest of the University running rough shod over environmental concerns.
—Dona Spring,
Berkeley City Council Member

After nearly six hours of public hearing, debate before a crowd of nearly 300 people, the Berkeley City Council voted early yesterday morning to recommend against university development on People's Park.
—Chris O'Sullivan, *Daily Cal* **Mar. 16, 1989**

To preserve the legacy of People's Park and as a mitigation for the university's development on campus and in the South Campus area, The planning commission policy platform, as amended by City Councilmember Don Jelinek, states with regard to the property, "The entire People's Park site should be transferred to the City of Berkeley or its designee, to be maintained as open space and as a monument to the legacy it represents"...The policy goes on to "exclude (the construction on the lot of) any housing, commercial, university or other institutional facilities."
—Roya Camp, *Berkeley Voice,*
Mar. 16, 1989

 I strongly support acquring People's Park — for the people, by the people and of the people. Until we secure that land it will be subject to University mismanagement and the threat of inappropriate development. Look at the history of park management. We can do much better, but only if we have control over the park. The way we get control is by owning the park."
—Maudelle Shirek,
Jan. 1996

"The Three Dorothies" meet: Dorothy Walker from UC,
Dorothy Eastor, a hills resident and
Dorothy Legaretta, from the People's Park Council

Joan Wallner, left, an outsider from Chicago was hired by the City to run the Rec program on their leased portion of the Park in the mid 1990's.

It's spring at People's Park. The grass is green and projects completed during the winter months have added tangible improvements: a new patio, improved walkways, retaining walls that prevent erosion and drainage problems, an enclosure to screen trash containers, planters crowded with flowers. In addition to these is a hard-working site coordinator who has embraced People's Park with enthusiasm..."I want to make this flower bloom," says Devin Woolridge, part of UC Berkeley's Office of Community Relations staff. He scans the park grounds from his office on the site. "It's not all milk and honey yet, but it's slowly getting better."

—D. Lyn Hunter, communityrelations. berkeley.edu Spring 2002

Over the years, university groundskeepers have ripped out benches, children's play equipment, bulletin boards, signs, even logs they didn't like. In 1976, they demolished a public water fountain as an unauthorized permanent structure. More recently, they have torn out foundations for permanent toilets (provocatively laid, it is true, by Mike Delacour's First Day of Spring Committee).

—Paul Rauber, "Field of Dreams"
***East Bay Express*, May 12, 1989**

Devin Woolridge, Irene Hegarty, Glenda Rubin

To the Chancellor:
"The true issue hasn't been touched yet," Palmer said. "There is over whelming student-faculty support for the park...We want to know if the university will respond to what we are asking. We don't want to hear what you're planning. That's not what we're saying. I think the issue involved is if the university community is really going to be a community. How the hell is anyone (in the administration) going to know if we're going to object to a plan unless there's some way of consulting students and finding out? ...How do we stop this violence from occurring again and again? We must start talking about opening up the decision-making processes from which we're now barred. You can't plan ten years ahead for students. You must talk about what students want now."

—Charles Palmer, then ASUC President May 26, 1969 KPFA

To the University, the non-student "street people" represent a dangerous alternative to which the students gravitate, drawn out of their carefully constructed academic orbit....The University feared the park not because it was monopolized by hard-core radical street people, but precisely because it brought together all kinds of people—related and united them. And the University was appalled by the non-students not because, as it is fond of charging, "all they want to do is to destroy." Such nihilism is hardly magnetic. The fear is that they will create, will establish a life-syle that is more satisfying than the work-a-day straight life. The fear is that their lifestyle will succeed. That also was the threat of the park. It was there. It was real. Utopian aspirations can be wistfully dismissed, but the park was not pie-in-the-sky.

—Robert Scheer, "Dialectics of Confrontation: Who Ripped off the Park", *Ramparts*, Fall 1969

This crisis did not start because reasonable people came in from the street to discuss possible uses of the University. Rather they occupied it, they claimed it, declared their contempt for its legal ownership and announced their intention to resist every effort of the University to possess it.

—(Chancellor) Roger Heyns, May 26, 1969, interview on KPFA

Well it is still a free speech area. When they whited, or greened out, the slogans, "democratize the regents" you can see how uptight they are on free speech, uptight on having the truth come out. So you can see how they're on the edge, they're vulnerable.

—Michael Delacour, interview Jan. 17, 2007

Ever since it has been a fight over the de jure university title and the de facto activist (lately homeless) title.

—Brook Schaaf, *DailyCal* Mar 3, 2000

"(People's Park) is every bit as important to some people as the Statue of Liberty," Spring said. "I sincerely hope that the students will choose a park. The area is so densely developed that we need some open space."...Spring said the park functions as spatial relief for the overcrowded area of Berkeley. "A developer is normally required to dedicate open space when the area is developed," Spring said. "People's Park is an open-space mitigation of the dense development brought to the Southside."

—*Daily Cal*, Mar. 7, 2000

The University has adopted a plan of action that one might call an "anti-Park policy". This policy has generally been carried out through consistant (sic) little subtle acts to discourage people from using and enjoying the park....In the spring on 1981, the U.C. Police Department printed an "official notice" in the Daily Californian: OFFICIAL NOTICE: To all students and others who reside in the south campus area re: Dangers in People's Park. Students and others who reside in the south campus area should be aware of the dangers in People's Park. Whenever possible, they should avoid walking through or alongside the park in their travels to and from campus, especially during nighttime hours . (D.C. 3/9/81)

— Howard S. Naness "The University's Role", Mar 7, 1983, Bancroft Library

The University of California was and IS a complete bastion of establishment rule, if that's what you want to call it, if you want to call it the rule of the big business interests, the capitalists, the power elite in our society and so to the extent to which we continue to care about the legacy of the park, to me it's a legacy of fighting the university. John Yoo, who was convicted by world opinion of being a war criminal, continues to be a faculty member in a school which teaches people to uphold the rule of law. Is there anything more absurd? Or you see BP, and major drug companies coming in and subverting the university to their research interest, their money making interest around bio-fuels or drugs or bio-engineered substances, plants, animals and so on. So, the fight isn't over and hopefully we will all continue in that fight as long as we breathe.

—Dan Siegel, 40th Anniversary Founders Forum, April 24, 2009

Above all, it came to represent one of the very few victories of ordinary Berkeleyites against the University; to be able to stroll the Park was to be able to remind yourself that sometimes you can win against the machine.... Many older people also felt that UC kept trying to get the Park back to attempt to finally erase its shame over the Free Speech Movement and the bloody-minded and lethal way it had supressed free speech and democracy during the sixties and seventies.

—www.pandemonia.com/pandemonia/occupation/ explanation.htm

The City and University created an "Advisory Committee" to recommend "rules" intended to govern People's Park. None of the members of said committee were appointed by the users of People's Park, by the garden caretakers of People's Park, by People's Park Council, or by any other community based group, other than by the City and University....With all due respect to the members thereof, this committee lacks the legitimate authority to impose rules upon People's Park without the consent of the governed. People's Park represents a unique experiment in user development, spontaneous creativity, community control and direct democracy.
—**People's Park Council Open Letter, June 18, 1991**

What if the City Did the Right Thing?
1. Buy the Park.
2. Bring up Derby Creek.
3. Promote People's Park nationally for its
a) rich history of Free Speech
b) community gardening
c) rare and native plant offerings
d) wonderful music concerts
e) a beautiful newly-restored creek.
What would the Benefits Be?
1. Peace in the Southside.
(The City does not share U.C.'s vendetta against the Park.)
2. Empty shops on Telegraph would find tenants given peace in the Southside.
3. Increase in City revenue due to increase in shopping from locals and tourists due to national promotion. We want peace! It could happen! Please think about it!
—**David Nadel, www.peoplespark.org**

Unfortunately for the University of California with its massive corporate-military contracts, People's Park has a soul that can never be extinguished. It burns in the hearts of all of us. It is the understanding that building a healthy community begins with laying your foundations on the bedrock of peace...The University only pretends to own that land; it is yours.
—**Arthur Fonseca, "What is People's Park?"**

In an "unauthorized" cleanup of the park Tuesday morning, university police and facilities management officials removed five benches, a bulletin board, and three trees, just before a group of park supporters, including Berkeley City Councilmember Nancy Skinner, were to meet with (chancellor) Heyman.
—**Craig Anderson, Daily Cal, Feb. 13, 1985**

"Improvements" are the euphemisms for upcoming city and UC efforts to separate the park from its history and traditions. More of these are planned soon. "Advisory groups" and "ad-hoc committees" are the terms used to describe the perhaps disoriented citizens appointed to "implement" these non-user-developed changes, usually designed to alter traditional users and uses to "welcome" a less radical, less committed, more sports-oriented crowd.
—**Carol Denny, Slappsuit brochure 2006**

7-8-81 For the third time, UC police remove children's play equipment from PP —**From Bob Sparks Chronology, courtesy David Blackman**

When will UC finally recognize that People's Park is enchanted? This land will never be just another hunk of university real estate.
—**Norris Lyle, circa 1979**

Lessee and Lessor acknowledge that the following structures have historically existed on the Park, and are herein approved as acceptable structures on either the UC or City portions of People's Park. The Stage, two (2) bulletin boards, the Free Box, benches, the Tool Box, and a sign designating the park as People's Park (the historic sign has several signs on it, including but not limited to "Everyone Gets a Blister," "Bulldozer Alert," and "People's Park."

5.7 Currently Existing Uses. Lessee and Lessor acknowledge that the following uses of People's Park have historically been allowed on the Park, and that both parties agree that these activities shall be permitted to continue: Community gardening, informal recreation, the providing of meals and other human services, freedom of expression, freedom of religion, vigils, concerts, rallies, and other gatherings. —**City Council minutes Feb. 26, 1991 "13. Resolution authorizing a Lease Agreement with the Regents of the University of California for a portion of People's Park"**

For many people around the world, Berkeley is People's Park. —**Berkeley City Council member Alan Goldfarb, The Right to the City: Social Justice and the Fight for Public Space, Don Mitchell, Guilford Press, 2003**

For David Axelrod, a park gardener and member of the People's Park Council, the question shouldn't be when the university takes over the park but when "we take over the university and democratize the son-of-a-gun" ..."This is a beachhead for democracy and freedom--that's why they can't tolerate it," Axelrod said. "They want to take Mother Earth and incarcerate her. As long as the people have a say, we will hold this ground for Mother Earth."

–Tom Lochner

We put in swings and we planted trees
Laid down the plumbing and the flower seed
But late at night the University still
Came to destroy what they refused to build
     Don't they see that the spirit remains
     One they can't stop with their fiscal games
     We'll work and fight if the need arise
     To keep the Park green before our eyes
So tell me where does it go from here?
Can they own this land? Can they own the air?
And I swear no building will be seen
Where the land must stay forever green
Where the land must stay forever green

—Hali Hammer,
"Forever Green"

Students say "yes" to People's Park
More than 50 percent of the voters in the April 11-13 election cast "yes" ballots to an initiative asking, "Do you think the People's Park area should remain a park as opposed to having UCB explore alternative uses for the space/land?"

—*Berkeley Daily Planet*, April 22-23, 2000

Why is it that very few students know the incredible/tumultuous ongoing story of the Park? A working class neighborhood where Allen Ginsberg and friends used to frolic. The University's use of eminent domain to destroy that neighborhood. The resulting muddy unused lot being converted into a Park by the community on its own initiative. The destruction of that Park by the University, followed by Police and National Guard occupation of the city, including the use of live ammunition on demonstrators and observers. A helicopter indiscriminately spraying tear gas on a peaceful rally and the city at large. A prior ASUC referendum where the Park won by a landslide. The Park persevering. Free food. Music. Swings and slides. Trees. Gardens. The People's Café. The Free Box. Volleyball courts that were forced upon the public by the University and thus never used, but cost the public $2 million. Thousands of arrests. Martial law on numerous occasions. Hundreds of injuries. And sadly two human beings killed at the hands of police officers.

How many students have even spent time in the Park? Lounged on the grass and enjoyed the sun? Utilized the Free Speech stage? Played some ball? Threw a Frisbee? Just sat and talked with a stranger? Planted flowers? Ate nourishing free food? Again, I'd bet very few.

Could this be because the University sends a police officer to warn every new student at Orientation about the "dangers" of People's Park? That the UCPD releases constant propaganda about the supposed "criminal element" in the Park?

—**John Tanghe, "The truth about the university's referendum on People's Park"**, *Daily Cal* Opinion April 3, 2000

Yes, this is true. People's Park is not a place where most students feel safe. But the primary reason students don't hang out there is largely that, for decades, the university has discouraged them from using the park to its fullest potential. In 1981 the UC Police bought a full-page ad in The Daily Californian urging students to avoid it.

—**Paul Hogwarth**, *Daily Cal*, April 12, 1999

On January 25th, (1992) over 50 activists met at an event called the Berkley Peace Conference to discuss the situation in People's Park, University of California development issues, and their effect on Berkeley's well-being and quality of life...By unanimous consent the Peace Conference endorsed a statement of solidarity and support with students protesting fee increases at U.C....We consider our struggle against the wayward policies of U.C. to be strongly related to your protest against the outrageous fee increases imposed upon students.

—**Mark McDonald letter**

Concert one fine Sunday at the Park

Walking down Telegraph you turn at the mural... a green expanse unfolds to your right... a big sign tells you you've reached People's Park.

A few people you may have seen around campus are shooting hoops, throwing a Frisbee. But this is no ordinary park; amidst rare native California shrubs a couple weeds give an impression of wildness- someone with a long beard speaks from the wooden, homemade looking stage about God and the cosmos while two old men play chess.

You're not in Kansas (or Long Beach) anymore. You're in one of the most unique spaces on Earth; to some people the closest place to real freedom available.

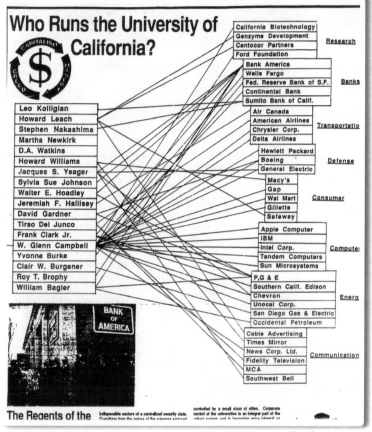

Who Runs the University of California?

The Regents of the

—*Slingshot 1991*

This slogan has been repeatedly painted out by UC staff promptly after appearing on the "Free Speech" Stage.

Why are the University of California regents so afraid of even discussing the idea of democracy within UC?...Six months ago I drafted a preliminary plan for democratizing the administration of the university and wrote to UC President David Gardner and to members of the Board of Regents, asking merely that this proposal be placed on the regents' agenda for public discussion. This request was repeatedly denied, without any cogent reason given for the refusal.

—**Charles Schwartz, Professor of Physics at UC Berkeley**

64 REASONS TO DEMOCRATIZE THE REGENTS OF THE UNIVERSITY OF CALIFORNIA

1. U.C. hires junk bond dealer, Micheal Milken, to teach corporate finance at UCLA. Milken was previously convicted of a felony and sentenced to ten years in prison. (Oakland Tribune, October 13, 1993)

2. The U.C. Regents, at a closed meeting, approve $797,000 payment plus $1,300,000-a-year pension for a total retirement package of $2.4 million for outgoing U.C. President David Pierpont Gardner. (S.F. Chronicle, July 19, 1993)

3. The State blames administrative mismanagement for U.C.'s decline. (Oakland Tribune, August 25, 1993)

4. U.C. student fees rise 128% over the last four years. (Daily Californian, October 8, 1993)

5. U.C. officials have predicted student fee increases of between $600 and $650 for the 1994-95 school year and each succeeding year. (Daily Californian, October 8, 1993)

6. U.C. has spent more than $800,000 for an infrequently used president's office in Irvine, including Wedgwood china, crystal brandy snifters, and $45,000 for two Iranian carpets.(Sacramento Bee, Aug. 27, 1992)

7. The U.C. managed nuclear weapons lab, Lawrence Livermore, will cost $442.476 million to cleanup and Los Alamos will cost $1.229 billion, according to the Department of Energy. (U.S. News and World Report, Dec. 14, 1992)

8. Two UCSF psychologists sued the university because of sexual harassment from their supervisor. They were then fired by U.C. (S.F. Weekly, sept. 29, 1993)

9. State Senator Tom Hayden reports that U.C. pays 1,700 employees salaries in excess of $100,000. U.C. has excluded 12,500 students since 1991. (Daily Californian, May 28, 1993)

10. Governor Wilson appoints close friend John Davies to the U.C. Board of Regents. Davies owns $1.3 million in property and had contributed $35,000 to Wilson's last campaign and inaugural.(S.F. Weekly, Jan. 27, 1993)

11. U.C. seeks fee increases for students and raises for 3 Chancellors. (S.F. Chronicle Nov. 14, 1992)

12. UCLA Chancellor Chareles E. Young received a low-interest loan of $995,000 to buy a $1 million house. (The Washington Spectator, June 1, 1993)

13. Legal fees paid to outside law firms have soared to $23 million, nearly doubling in the past three years. (S.F. Chronicle, July 23, 1993)

14. A Chico rancher received a $3 million settlement in a libel suit against U.C. after the university blamed him for the death of 500 of his prize cows. The rancher charged U.C. with deliberately covering up for state and federal officials who had poisoned his cows with pesticide.(S.F. Chronicle Aug. 14, 1992)

15. U.C. proposes a $9 million hazardous waste storage site in the hills above the U.C. campus at Berkeley, 2,000 feet from the Hayward earthquake fault.(Oakland Tribune Aug. 31 1993)

16. The inspector general of the Dept. of Energy reveals that the U.C. regents withheld information from the D.O.E. about an insider trading investigation involving Lawrence Livermore Laboratory, and proposes barring U.C. from doing business with the federal government. (Oakland Tribune, Jan. 15, 1993)

17. UCLA Chancellor Chuck Young billed the university $600 for a golf tournament. (Sacramento Bee, Aug. 27, 1992)

18. U.C. president David Gardner votes to keep $3.1 billion investments in South Africa. (Daily Californian, July 23, 1986)

19. U.C. Regents tried to downplay the $2.4 million Gardner deal. Transcripts show they were well aware of probable public outcry over the package. (S.F. Chronicle April 16, 1992)

20. U.C. patent officer, Carl Wooten steered contracts worth more than $367,000 to a longtime friend and former business partner. (S.F. Examiner, Aug. 8, 1993)

21. U.C. Senior Vice President, Ronald Brady, who arranged the $2.4 million deal for David Gardner, was given $181,000 paid leave, approved by Gardner. (Oakland Tribune, May 12, 1993)

22. U.C. is eliminating 1,000 jobs and cutting employees' pay by 5 percent. (Oakland Tribune, May 13, 1993)

23. Average personal wealth of Board of Regent members is over $700,000. (Sacramento Bee, July 26, 1992)

Ever since the University signed a $500 million deal with British Petroluem the "BP Bears" have been seen cheerleading through Park and Town.

CAL DOESNT PAY WORKERS LIVING WAGES

MEMORIALS

People's Park is nurtured by the blood, sweat and tears of many and some have really been a special part of the character and history of the Park over the years. The following is a tribute to some, though by no means all, of those who gave to the park community as a whole and have left the gift of their specialness in the history and soil of People's Park. Their work and time was unpaid, contributed freely for the betterment of the whole. May they be remembered.

JAMES RECTOR

One of my best friends and me were on a roof top during the riots there in Berkeley. I caught some buckshot, another friend was blinded and Jimmy died a few days later. He did not die for nothing, we took that park back for the people. I may be too old now to stand up to tear gas and such, I have to rely on you younger people to take my place and shout it shall be free, and remember James Rector!

— Mike Two Feathers
email to peoplesparkcommunity July 31, 2006

At first, of course, we didn't believe that they were shooting at unarmed people. "What the hell is that?" we asked each other. Somebody suggested it was rock salt. Then a group of four, five, or six police in the middle of the block raised their guns to shoot. "Buckshot!" somebody shouted. James Rector saw the policeman aiming at his face. He turned his back and began to run; he was too late. Three pellets caught him in the lower left back, and he crumpled onto the roof... I was standing beside him when he fell; again I still didn't believe that there had been any shooting; perhaps Rector had sprained his ankle. But when I got to him he couldn't breathe; and when I lifted up his jacket there were three bullet holes in his back.

— Michael Meo, witness to the shooting of James Rector, "James Rector, 25 —Died for People's Park"

The Daily Californian

Riot Victim Dies

National Guard Sweeps Onto Campus; Clouds of Tear Gas Spread in Plaza

Students to Vote

—from Mural on Haste St.

COWBOY KOGER

Cowboy Koger, a hero of People's Park, was the founder of the People's Park west-end community gardens. In the 1979 parking-lot occupation, he was the most prominent person in maintaining order. He made great efforts in mediating between people for People's Park on a grassroots level and official city and UCB powers.

In a society with much internal strife and warfare, Cowboy Koger died from getting shot in the head. A memorial service was held for him in People's Park.

For many years, a crude but respectful wooden plaque in tribute to Cowboy Koger was seen on the Haste-Street side of People's Park

—Sketch and words by B.N. Duncan

—courtesy B.N. Duncan and Jim Robinson

GYPSY CATANO

Gypsy Catano, long gone, was a street person, and a man of many parts -- known for being an activist, rogue, inspirational leader, violent alcoholic, outlaw, goof, and eccentric with a colorful, vital spirit.

—B.N. Duncan

STEW ALBERT

Local elections were coming up and Michael Delacour, the father of People's Park, recalled that, mostly in jest, I had once threatened to run for Sheriff of Alameda County. He wanted me to do it for real. It'll be a great protest campaign against what the Sheriff's Department did to us during People's Park.

It was cops from the Sheriff's Department who blazed a shotgun trail down Telegraph Avenue and killed James Rector. They wore blue uniforms and their long standing, Beatle-inspired, nickname was Blue Meanies.

**— Stew Albert
"Stew Albert Runs for Sheriff"
Berkeley 1970**

WHEREAS Stew Albert died at 3:20 AM on Monday morning, January 30th in Portland, Oregon, and WHEREAS, Stew Albert was a leader of the Vietnam Day Committee, an organizer of peace marches through the streets of Oakland and through the streets of Washington D.C. and through the streets of Chicago and through the streets around the Pentagon and through the streets of Berkeley and through the streets around People's Park,

and WHEREAS, Stew Albert was a prisoner at Santa Rita for his role in People's Park, was released and became a candidate for Sheriff of Alameda County in 1970, receiving 65,000 votes, carrying Berkeley by 10,000 votes,

and WHEREAS, Stew Albert was a co-founder of the Yippies and a friend of Jerry Rubin and a friend of Abbie Hoffman and a friend of Eldridge Cleaver and a friend of John Lennon and a friend of thousands who identified with the Movement,

and WHEREAS, Stew Albert was a target of J. Edgar Hoover and a target of Richard Nixon and a target of the FBI and the victor in a lawsuit against their harassment and an irrepressible critic of the unjust and the idiotic to the moment he died, addressing the power that rules us now, and WHEREAS, Stew Albert kept faith with the Movement and kept its spirit alive in his soul every day and served as the Movement's living historian and the Movement's living history lesson and the Movement's connection to new generation after new generation,

now THEREFORE, BE IT RESOLVED that the Oakland City Council proclaims Wednesday, February 1, 2006, the day of his memorial service, "Stew Albert Day" in the City of Oakland, in recognition of his contributions, his humor and his good sense, his decency and his faith in what can be, what must be and what will be.

**—Ignacio De La Fuente
President: Oakland City Council 2006**

DAVID NADEL

—Brenda Prager

Tile wall on Front of Ashkenaz

Every weekend he manned three tables in the park and passed out information about the crooked activities of the Board of Regents, routinely called 'Corporate Thugs' in his monthly editorials. The Regents ultimately SLAPP sued David to try to deactivate him, but it didn't work.

— Clay Geerdes Jan. 15, 1997
"David Nadel [1946-1996]"

Mr. David Nadel is the owner of the Ashkenaz Cafe in Berkeley, California. The University of California at Berkeley has litigation pending against Mr. Nadel for last year's incidents at People's Park. For nineteen years or more, David Nadel has acted in the true spirit of Berkeley, bringing people of all classes, races, cultures and ages together. The Peace & Justice Commission is recommending that Mr. Nadel be commended for his outstanding work and lifelong commitment to the causes of peace and social justice, multi-cultural folk, dance, music, literary programs, the innumerable political fund-raisers he has put on at Ashkenaz, for local organizations, a multitude of causes and for individuals including elected officials.

— Peace and Justice Commission

PROCLAMATION HONORING DAVID NADEL AND DECLARING THE WEEK OF JANUARY 14, 1997 TO JANUARY 21, 1997 AS DAVID NADEL WEEK

WHEREAS, David Nadel was honored by the City of Berkeley in 1993 as a Tzaddic (Righteous One) for his outstanding work and for his lifetime commitment to the causes of peace, justice and respect for human rights; and

WHEREAS, as a political activist stubbornly prin-

cipled and deeply committed to his beliefs, Dave Nadel's gift to his community was sharing what he thought life ought to be while working to make life what it should be; and

WHEREAS, the support for his community that David Nadel gave in such a gracious, generous manner--the list of over 250 causes that have raised funds at Ashkenaz is a catalogue of Berkeley activit--was reciprocated with a massive show of support in the defense of Ashkenaz when it was endangered by the lawsuit brought against him by the University Of California Regents; and

WHEREAS, David Nadel was a longtime peace advocate who supported a People's Park independent of the University of California Regents and proceeded to follow governmental procedures to change the composition of the Board of Regents by having them democratically elected; and..

— City of Berkeley Proclamation

David Nadel, nightclub owner and Berkeley activist who championed the preservation of People's Park and rights for its denizens, died at Highland Hospital Saturday, two days after he was shot in the head. He was 50...He enjoyed a reputation in the East Bay as a pacifist and Berkeley radical. He fought for People's Park regulars and published a newsletter critical of powerful people and institutions. (UC Scandal Sheet)

— Examiner Obituaries
David Nadel, club owner and activist

And let's remember that if it wasn't for park supporters who marched, rallied, sat-in, got arrested, and got beaten there would be sports courts all across the open space, green-grass, and public assembly areas of the park; and the Free Speech Stage would have been torn out and replaced by the toilets.

A stand against corporate expansion in 1969—a stand against corporate (UC) expansion now. You all know it. If UC can dominate, confiscate, tear up the turf, threaten dorms, and one way or another (with Mayor Hancock leading UC's charge) ruin People's Park, they'll be very hard to stop in the rest of Berkeley. Think about it. In the '20s UC ripped off the hillside and rammed in the football stadium, in the '40s UC ripped off Telegraph Avenue from Sather Gate to Bancroft Way, in the late '70s UC

continued on next page

gobbled up the sixty-acre School for the Deaf and Blind, in 1991 UC took all of Presentation High School, and now comes their attempt to retake and decimate People's Park.

If the park goes there'll be no stopping UC—the insatiable beast that covets Berkeley. Stand up for Free Speech, for user-development, for open space, and for basic needs, Stand up for People's Park!

—Letter from David Nadel,
EastBay Express, **Dec. 18, 1992**

Carved volleyball court pillar planted in south park.

BOB SPARKS

Bob Sparks Died April 30, 1995
from high blood pressure induced
Cardiovascular disease.

BOB SPARKS MEMORIAL DEMO

SPEAKERS & MUSIC
LEE GOLAND
&
MAX VENTURA
STARTS AT
HO CHI MINH PARK
UP HILLEGASS
TO PEOPLE'S PARK

MAY 19, 1995

—courtesy David Blackman

—courtesy David Axelrod

Local political activist Bob Sparks began a hunger-strike this week to protest "injustices occurring in the city of Berkeley," including a lawsuit against him by the University of California and the city's proposed anti-panhandling law. "I'm doing the most personal thing I can do to protest (these injustices), and that's put my life on the line," he said.

— Will Harper
"Sparks protests life in Berkeley
Long-time local initiates a fast"

The cops eventually secured the courts, but that first chainsaw massacre remains one of the all time greatest moments in protest history. Really, people were high on that action for weeks. Bob Sparks has been charged with the deed, a great honor. If he is the one, it would be great symbolic free speech, as well. During the Haste St. Massacre, a gang of cops set upon him as he sat non-violently on the street. They beat him Rodney King style for a long time. Later, they clubbed the people who carried Bob towards the ambulance on a stretcher. Really, it was horrible what the cops were doing during those initial days and nights of police rioting. For Bob to raise up from that bearing and end up being the first one to hack down a net post would be a perfect symbolic way of saying that you can't stop dissent with brutality.

— C. beck, "Save People's Park
A work in progress", 1992

JUDY FOSTER

—*Lydia Gans*

—*Lydia Gans*

Judy was inspiration, mentor, mother, wise woman, caring; her heart opening wide to see the beauty in even the most twisted of us, supporting and urging us to be all we are. She worked hard her whole life, cooking amazing meals to share the sacred food with thousands. Her guiding light created "Gourmet Tuesdays", the best meal in town, Food Not Bombs in People's Park. Judy lived large, joyfully and bravely. She spoke her mind and didn't worry much about the "rules". She laughed, sang, danced and showed how to live a life full of love. Viva Judy.

—ed. Jan. 21, 2009

East Bay Food Not Bombs has been a healing, positive part of our progressive culture. And we do it on a shoe-string...All over the world, sharing food together is an acknowledgement of common humanity, an act of peace. We do not just serve "the homeless", we serve any-one who comes to eat; we serve ourselves... Love Judy

—Food Not Bombs donation request letter

—*Lydia Gans*

JONATHAN MONTIGUE

—*Lydia Gans*

I gladly describe myself as "the last Barrington shaman" ...I joined what I will call the Thornberry Generation which is comprised of anarchists, counterculturists, sundry left-wingers, eco-pagans and existentialists of all kinds. You can join too if you want.

—Jonathan Montague, *Slingshot* **Spring 1992**

JOHN MICHAEL JONES

John Michael Jones, an activist who helped found People's Park in 1969, received a standing ovation from about half of the audience...Jones said the university has ignored concerns of people who use the park.

—Shandra Martinez, 'Town Meeting' draws few students, Call to destroy courts lauded", *Daily Cal* Sept. 9, 1991

DONA SPRING

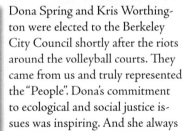

Dona Spring and Kris Worthington were elected to the Berkeley City Council shortly after the riots around the volleyball courts. They came from us and truly represented the "People". Dona's commitment to ecological and social justice issues was inspiring. And she always remained open to the Park community and the values it holds. **—ed.**

ELI YATES

—courtesy Christopher McKinney

Eli, beloved mucisian and sweet spirit, blessed the Park with song, care and action. **—ed.**

BOB NICHOLS

I too drifted away but became reinvolved just over a year ago when the latest assault on the park began. Rather than "schizophrenic homeless and drugged-out losers," I found a community of dedicated citizens, housed and homeless, working together gardening, feeding people and organizing for political empowerment while constantly being harassed by the police. I have been arrested for daring to stand silent vigil on a sidewalk.

As a result of my contact with People's Park, I have become more involved in local government issues throughout Berkeley than ever in my life. I have realized that freedom and human rights need to be defended at home as well as abroad. This is surely the crux of the "freedom movement born in Berkeley" rather that an insult to it. **—Robert Nichols, letter "People's Park"**

JON READ

John Read was a landscape architect that became involved in the birth of the Park, bringing crucial expertise and energy. He remained involved in the Park, spearheading the planting of the street trees on Haste Street in the 1990's.

LARRY

Larry was active in Food Not Bombs, save KPFA and other local causes. He also participated in the historical WTO protest in Seattle in 1999. **—ed.**

—photo Lydia Gans

HAL CARLSTAD

Hal Carlstad was an amazing inspiration, forever standing up for justice and the rights of people. Always at the important protests of the day, he was arrested countless times for standing up for his beliefs. He was involved in the "People's Pad", a community living experimental offshoot of the Park. **—ed.**

THUNDER

Thunder painted this on the Park bathroom just a week or two before he died.

Thunder was a Native American organizer helping to free Leonard Peltier, a member of Berkeley Liberation Radio, and an activist for Berkeley Homeless for the preservation of People's Park.
—Redwood Mary, interview, Mar 14, 2009

CLAIRE BURCH

Claire was an amazingly prolific documenter of the unique aspects of our community and did a lot of works about people of People's Park. Her videos and books include; *People's Park of Berkeley: Then and Now, Country Joe McDonald: Concerts at People's Park, Hello Goodbye Bob Sparks, Homeless in the Nineties, What Really Killed Rosebud?*, and *The People's Park Anniversary Series.* **—ed.**

B.N. DUNCAN

—Greg Jalbert

B.N. Duncan cared greatly for People's Park and the people therein. His artwork of cartoon versions of local characters graces the south wall of the bathroom in People's Park. He co-published the Telegraph Street Calendar appreciating the local diversity. Duncan also gave generously to this book project, providing neatly labeled envelopes of photos, artwork and interviews. His sweet concern will be greatly missed. **—ed.**

He was such a quintessential weirdo (at least on the surface) that it usually took people a while to get Duncan. He was a guy that went out of his way not to try to be lovable and charming. But it was amazing how many people he ended up charming anyway... I used Duncan as sort of a barometer of people. If they could tell Duncan was cool, then they were cool with me.
—Ace Backwards, June 30, 2009

JOHN COOPER

—*Mark Koehler, Berkeley Voice 5/18/89*

That (Catholic Worker) cafe was there till the spring, at least 6 months and then all of a sudden they jacked it out of there and nobody could stop them.
I think that's what actually killed John was the fact that they took the Cafe out.
—Michael Delacour, interview Jan. 17, 2007

MICHAEL ROSSMAN

Perhaps the most significant feature of Michael was that he embodied the ebullient vigor of the spirit of "the movement" - the deep belief that everyone deserved a richer, more integrated life in communal harmony. He was unafraid to push boundaries, to challenge stereotypes, and to accept new ideas.
—Lincoln Cushing, Docs Populi, May 17, 2008

Others to be remembered:
Mario Savio
Hida Judelson
Chris Delvecciao
Charlene Paul
Bruce "A"
Fred Lupke
Kevin Freeman
Jay Wiseman
John Burk
Ella the Nature Dog
Lucy the Dog

People's Park

David Nadel
Memorial Ash

Fred Cody
Memorial Redwood Grove

John Lennon
Memorial Plum Tree

Bob Sparks
Memorial Pineapple Guava

Judy Foster
Memorial
Lemon Tree

John Cooper Catholic Worker
Memorial Rose

Ash Tree Honoring
Raven's Baby, Nigel

Betsy's Roses

Martin Luther King Jr.
Memorial Cherry Tree

Ella the Dog
Elder(Ella)berry

Almond Tree
Memorial for Acacia Tree
that was cut down by UC

Rosebud Denovo's
Memorial Rose Bush

LET 1000 PARKS BLOOM

As the rage and tear gas settled, so did the dream of People's Park. But its ideas spread like a mycelium: threadlike, underground, popping up as mushrooms where conditions are favorable. The ideas and the experience traveled to places far and wide, carried deep in the hearts of the participants. —**Sim Van der Ryn,** *Design for Life,* **2005**

—Prentice Brooks, "People's Park Protest" May 26, 1969
The Oakland Tribune Collection, the Oakland Museum of Californa. Gift of ANG Newspapers.

—Elihu Blotnick, Ramparts 69

—Pierre La Plant

After People's Park was suppressed, gardens began popping up all over Berkeley, most notably over the recently cleared land for the BART tunnel. "People's Park Annex" was planted by thousands of folks unable to give up on the dream. The city of Berkeley and BART worked with the groundswell and the Annex still lives today as Berkeley's Ohlone Park. The idea of reclaiming the land, getting back to the garden, and creating community parks spread to other parts of the country and world.

LET A THOUSAND PARKS BLOOM

—Gil Madrid

—Prentice Brooks, "People's Park Protest" May 26, 1969"
The Oakland Tribune Collection,
the Oakland Museum of California. Gift of ANG Newspapers

—Pierre La Plant

INSTANT NEWS SERVICE
1703 GROVE, BERKELEY 841-9480
COURTESY: PEOPLE'S PRESS SYNDICATE

Vol. 1, No. 9   Page 1   Monday, May 26, 1969

People's Stew will be served every day at 6:00 pm at People's Park Annex, Hearst and Grant Streets. Even while we are fighting to regain the first People's Park, we are building another one. Construction started yesterday in mid-afternoon. By evening, sod had been laid, flowers, gardens, and small trees planted, children's play equipment installed, a bandstand erected, and a barbeque pit dug. We will gather every afternoon to continue building this park.

There will be music. The best music in the world is the music played

—Harold Adler

—Grover Wichersham

PEOPLE'S PARK No. 2 . . . was planted about 2 p.m. yesterday at Grove and Hearst, the first of a number of parks that sprung up throughout the day.

—Photo by GROVER WICKERSHAM

Annex the day after the 1/18/70 planting of trees. Previously, on 5/30/69, we planted flowers, got together, and marched. Several of the trees are still growing in 2008. Also, the colorful jungle gym in the Annex (now called Ohlone Park) is still there.
—Pierre La Plant

—Pierre La Plant

165

OTHER PEOPLE'S PARKS

People's Park, Justin Morrill College, Michigan State University-Lansing —Kevin Fulton

During the spring of 1970, a "People's Park" sprang up in the quad area south of the Red Cedar River ...Residents pitched tents (and at least one tipi) or set up improvised lean-to's. The area (also dubbed "Free") remained the scene of a persistent resident population, daily passers-through, and regular gatherings through the remainder of that turbulent spring term.

People's Park, Tacoma Washington

People's Park Bloomington Indiana

Oregon State University People's Park

In 1972, students lobbied Oregon State Universtiy administration to create a park space at the site of the recently demolished administration building. Beginning in 2002, the construction of Kelley Engineering Center prompted the relocation of the park to its current location just west of Gilkey Hall.

EARTH PEOPLES PARK

1970: Helped initiate an experiment of buying back the earth and deeding it back to itself. Purchased 590 acres in northern Vermont and called it Earth People's Park.

—www.wavygravy.net

...buy land, throw away the deed, open it to anyone and call it Earth People's Park. Hold an earth-warming festival and ecological world's fair—all free.... Paul Krassner, Tom Law, Milan Melvin, Ken Kesey, Mama Cass Elliot, and the Hog Farm traveling communal circus led by Hugh Romney fanned out to sell the idea. They asked everyone who had been at Woodstock in body or spirit to contribute a dollar. ...Hugh Romney, calling himself Wavy Gravy, in an aviator suit, sheepskin vest, and a Donald Duck hat, spoke on television about simplicity, community, and harmony with the land.

—www.saradavidson.com

We raised the money and did the purchase. That was the last left hand turn in America, in Norton Vermont. Then the feds tried to seize the property about 10-15 years ago. With the help of Howard Dean, who was Governor of Vermont then and Roz Payne,.. we were able to turn it into a State Park. I was there for the opening, where we did a big concert there with the Holy Modal Rounders and David Bromberg. And people built houses there and lived there and it was fine for 20 years. And of course it was inspired by People's Park.

—Wavy Gravy, interview Mar. 5, 2009

THE 1991 ANNEX

—C. beck

In mid-September, park activists took the offensive, occupying a nearby vacant lot where a suspicious fire had destroyed a transient hotel. The concrete lot sprung to life, with flowers, landscaped paths, benches and impromptu art work. Because the land is privately owned and the owner has not filed a complaint, the police have been powerless to intervene so far, but the authorities are clearly incensed at the "annex," a stark symbol of what the park's defenders can do at no cost to the taxpayers.

— George Franklin, "Z" Magazine, Dec. 1991

Uninterrupted by authorities, about 50 people worked all day Saturday and Sunday to convert the rubble strewn vacant lot at the intersection of Telegraph Avenue and Haste Street into a green area speckled with young trees and flower beds..."These things tend to be organically executed, so it's still in transition," a participant calling himself Freedom Fighter Jim said. "The idea just got planted in the people's mind and yesterday the people just got up and started doing it."

— Ralph Jennings, "Activists find new garden Annex property at burned hotel site"

Shortly after the regents' and city's cops took over People's Park for the scabs, The People felt a need to build another Park, a People's Park annex. The fence surrounding the vacant lot at the corner of Haste and Tele., half a block from People's Park, had been torn down by protesters during the initial police riot on black Wed.. This lot became People's Park Annex. It was a typical, People's Park, "Everyone gets a blister," type of action. It seemed like everyone was pitching in to turn this empty dirt lot into a beautiful Park. They came with picks, shovels, and rakes. People worked really hard, bringing in all manner of donated materials. **—C.beck**

—*courtesy of David Axelrod*

I'm breathing a great sigh of relief that it (People's Park) still has its existence after all the trouble we have been through.
—Andrea Moore,
"People's Park Speak-Out, interviews in 1993 and 1994 by B.N Duncan"

You've pushed us to the edge of your civilization, here against the sea in Berkeley, then you pushed us into a square block area we called PEOPLE'S PARK. It was the last thing we had to defend, this square block of sanity amidst all of your madness.....Because those of us who have walked through PEOPLE'S PARK were able to say like Paul Krassner— "I have seen the Revolution, and it works."

People will still gather around the primordial fire of PEOPLE'S PARK, tabernacle of the Work, to laugh and sing after a day spent working together.

And the bitter, the disgusted, the sick, and the wretched will still huddle together on that square block of land behind the Med and the Forum, along Telegraph Avenue. And if in passing you should happen to peek at us through the bushes, you will find us still....smiling.
—Tari, "After the Fire"
***Berkeley BARB*, May 16-22, 1969**

People's Park is the birthplace of modern communitarian ecology movement. It deserves to remain a force of nature, a fractal wonderland. Always evolving. Like many hands on a Ouija board you gotta trust it to spell out good words. The Park is Nature. We are the Park...There has been an in-dwelling wisdom there for almost 40 years since we cleaned it up. It doesn't need the other kind of cleaning up. It doesn't need to be cemented over, fenced in, plaqued to death. Just let the people keep coming and working on it and being.
—Wendy Schlesinger, interview Sept. 22, 2007

Julia Vinograd   *—courtesy of David Axelrod*

People's Park
Is this it? people ask.
looking vaguely cheated
at the flat lawn, a few trees
broken asphalt, dealers and healers,
lovers and shovers, drunks
and hunks of time
where bummers and summers sprawl.
"is this all?"
  Yes
  and sometimes
  it's
  enough.   **—Julia Vinograd, 1981**

I was never comfortable there, only happy.
—Julia Vinograd, 1976

Julia Vinograd   *—Lydia Gans*

Though its "public" status remains ambiguous to this day (given UC's legal title to the land), the political importance of the park as a public space rests on its status as a taken space. By wresting control of the park from the state, park activists, to one degree or another, and over a period of more than 30 years, have held at bay those who wish to impose on the land a very different conceptualization of public space...The very survival of People's Park in the face of so many pressures to "reform" it is testimony to the ability of ongoing struggle to maintain a certain vision of public space...More and more the spaces of the modern city are being produced for us rather than by us.
—Don Mitchell, *The Right to the City: Social Justice and the Fight for Public Space*,
Guilford Press, 2003

The park now is... really nice actually. I was there earlier this week doing some homework. The east (sic) end is full of flower and vegetable gardens tended by various people from the community. Some folks live there near the trees on either end. The free box is still there for anyone to donate things that they don't need to anyone who does need them. Near the free box are the "Free Speech Stage," (which is just a wooden platform where bands sometimes play and where speakers address crowds from) and the Free Speech Bulletin Board. The whole middle of the park is a pretty big span of really soft grass. There's play equipment and picnic benches nestled between paths and clearings in the trees (all of which are gorgeous.) There is even a tire swing, which is damn cool. On the north side of the park, there are basketball courts. There were about 20 guys playing there when I went the other day. The public restrooms to the west of the courts are painted all in murals, and on the inside, someone has written the history of the park for everyone to read.
—ifeeldizzy, everything2.com Sun Sept. 17, 2000

And then of course it came to be a whole confrontation between the people who ran the University who were very rich men who represented, as much as possible, the ruling circles of the State of California and the kinds of things that they wanted to do to the University and to education and to the neighboring communities, a struggle between that and some kind of, for lack of a better term, countercultural dream.
—Frank Bardacke, interview Nov. 30, 2006

—Courtesy of Berkeley Architectural and Heritage Association

—courtesy of David Axelrod

—George Kaufmann, courtesy of Berkeley Architectural and Heritage Association

—Harold Adler

169

People's Park
7 months after
the May 1969
protests...Then
a parking lot,
open for use, but
NOBODY used
it, as further
protest. Not
even UC staff
used it. Go Figure. It was now "sacred ground".

—Pierre La Plant,   Parking Lot 1969

—B.N. Duncan

—John Jekabson (both)

For 22 years People's Park has stood as a victory over corporate expansion into our community by the University of California. The University is run by The Regents—primarily rich, white, male, property-owners who sit on the Board of Directors of Lockheed, Boeing, Hewlett Packard, General Electric, Exxon, Chevron, Arco, IBM, General Motors etc, etc, etc. Just as these same corporations went to the Persian Gulf to control the resources there, and to erase the defeat of corporate expansion into Viet Nam, they now are coming to People's Park to control the resources there (open space), and to erase our 22 year victory over U.C. expansion.

Go to People's Park...often...use the Park for active and passive recreation, garden in the Park (it's your Park), donate clothes and food to the needy in the Park, hold your meetings there, enhance the food, clothing, and medical programs already coming out of the Park ...add your energy to the Park!

—David Nadel
"Defend People's Park"

Berkeley, Calif.— For some young students here, it is hard to imagine that the shabby vacant lot populated by homeless people is really the legendary People's Park, the lasting physical manifestation of the storied 60's.

—Katherine Bishop,   *NYT* July 5, 1991

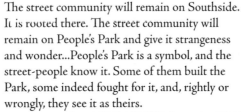

The street community will remain on Southside. It is rooted there. The street community will remain on People's Park and give it strangeness and wonder...People's Park is a symbol, and the street-people know it. Some of them built the Park, some indeed fought for it, and, rightly or wrongly, they see it as theirs.

—from Catholic Worker pamphlet

The park recently celebrated its 34th year as liberated territory. It has not been without its problems, but it has always remained as a symbol and a reality. Long Live People's Park!

—Ron Jacobs,
"Showdown in the Counterculture Corral"
www.counterpunch.org
May 23, 2003

—Jane Scheer

—Jane Scheer

Judy and Hawk
— Jim Robinson

—Jane Scheer

—courtesy Jim Robinson

People's Park is the dream from which Berkeley cannot awake. Twenty years ago Monday they put a fence around it, tore up the flowerbeds, shot a man dead in an attempt to end what one city councilmember called a "gypsy dreamland." Two decades later, the reality is crime-ridden, feared, and avoided, but the dream persists. People's Park, the way it was at its creation, has become part of Berkeley's political mythology: a communitarian Eden where Adam delved and Eve span, and all of the city joined to make a wasteland grow...Had it not been aborted by the university, it's likely that the experiment would have gone the way of so many other idealistic projects of the '60's, disintegrating amid power struggles, suspicion, and neglect. But...maybe not. Unrealized potential is part of the tragic allure of People's Park. If it hadn't been for the foolish bureaucracy of the University of California, the brutal violence of the Alameda County Sheriff's Department, the agents provocateurs, the implacable opposition of the political establishment, it just might have worked. After all, back then a new society was being built as well as a new park, and everything seemed possible. But the dream was stolen, and Berkeley has sought in vain ever since to recapture it.

—Paul Rauber, "Field of Dreams",
East Bay Express, **May 12, 1989**

"I think the park is significant. It demonstrated some important principles ... citizenry, community, grass roots action and the plausible civil defiance of undue authoritarian forces."
**—Christopher Kohler,
interview, 2007**

Paul Kilduff: You're still pretty involved with People's Park—should it just stay the way it is?
Wavy Gravy: No, nothing should stay the way that it is. Otherwise it would die. But there's a lot of spirit in People's Park. The gardeners are very dedicated. They've put in lots of time. It could be mo bettah. The city should buy it, and it should be policed and the drug dealers should be tossed out. There's a difference between scoundrel, cretin-pig swine and a poor homeless person. They should get treatment. They should not be in People's Park causing problems.
—The Monthly, October 2000

— David Axelrod

—David Blackman

—art by Eddie Monroe

BERKELEY, Calif. — On days when the sun looks kindly on it, People's Park can seem like a quaint little town.

So many different types of people protested the official over-reaction to the park— 30,000 people (in a city of 100,000) marched to protest Gov. Ronald Reagan's order to send in 2,000 National Guard troops with rifles, hoses and tear gas— that People's Park became a worldwide symbol of the power of community.

But that was then. Since 1972, when activists tore down the chain-link fence the university had erected around it, People's Park has become the refuge for a cadre of fringe characters. Drug dealers and users, has-been hippies and would-be hippies, panhandlers on break and several societies of homeless people dug in their heels. Just about everyone else scattered to a more congenial park two blocks away, or to the cafes around the corner, or the campus plazas. In short, anywhere but here.
**—Evelyn Nieves "A Landmark of the 60's, People's
Park Defies Transformation"
www.anusha.com/peoplesp.htm**

No matter what you say about People's Park it's likely to be partially right and completely wrong. People see it through their own prism.
**—Irene Hegarty, UC's Community Relations
People's Park laison, mid 1990's-2009, June 25, 2009**

—Lydia Gans *—Brenda Preger* *—Lydia Gans*

The park is no longer a symbol of unspoiled nature, a sylvan glade, a patch of welcoming turf, a haven for "the People." It is, instead, a filthy and inhospitable den, a place for drug dealing and drug use, a place mothers are afraid to take children at noon, a place where wary eyes follow outsiders who venture in.

In the minds of many Berkeley residents who once were willing to fight for the symbol, People's Park has lost its meaning. Worse, it has come to symbolize failed imagination and capitulation to mob rule.

— Belinda Taylor,
***Oakland Tribune* editorial Sept. 20, 1992**

But more important, many of us Berkeley residents are continuing to plant, keep the park clean, meet our friends there, and take a break while shopping on Telegraph Avenue....Yes, thanks to Reagan and Bush there are more homeless everywhere now than in the late '60's. I've befriended some of them in the park, and learned much from them. I encourage you to do the same. Come with me.

—Rita Wilson, Berkeley,
***Oakland Tribune*
letter Sept. 1992**

A few blocks down Telegraph Avenue, then one block east brought me to this peaceful scene, an urban park. At first glance it was hard to imagine that this piece of land had been at the center of the most deadly confrontation in Berkeley's radical past. But look again, and the signs were everywhere. At the edge of the lawn in this picture you can see a bandstand. On the side someone had written these words: "Free Speech. Truth is a Virus. Food not Bombs."
— "A Grassy Park" www.narhist.ewu.edu

If you walk five blocks north from the Whole Foods in Berkeley along Telegraph Ave and then turn at Dwight, you'll soon come to a trash-strewn patch of grass and trees dotted with the tattered camps of a few dozen homeless people. Mostly in their fifties and sixties, some still affecting hippie styles of hair and dress, these men and women pass much of their days sleeping and drinking, like so many of the destitute everywhere. Here, though, they also spend time tending scruffy little patches of flowers and vegetables—a few stalks of corn, some broccoli plants gone to seed. People's Park today is the saddest of places, a blasted monument to sixties' hopes that curdled a long time ago. And yet, while the economic and social distances separating the well-heeled shoppers cruising the aisles at Whole Foods from the unheeled homeless in People's Park could not be much greater; the two neighborhood institutions are branches of the same unlikely tree.

— Michael Pollan "From People's Park to Petaluma Poultry", *Omnivore's Dilemma*, 2006

What I remember—what comes through the turgid prose of my journal—is the calm at the core of my excitement, terror, thrill. There was defiance and danger, sure. But there was also the sense of being right. Of being on the side of decency and justice..., a justice so pure and so simple that I could not imagine it being fairly denied... We were right. People's Park, Berkeley California, May 15, 1969, and the weeks that followed. The best days of my youth.

—Guy Lillian,
***Challenger* #2, winter of 1995**

—Claire Burch *— Claire Burch 1979*

—art by Moby

—*Food Conspiracy Cookbook, 1974*

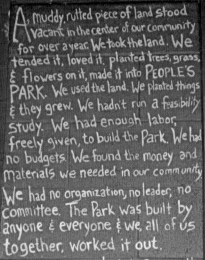

173

—Crow

—Lydia Gans

—Crow

A diverse pack of students marched from People's Park down Telegraph and Shattuck Avenues chanting "No war on Iraq! Let's have a peace talk!" and hoisting signs to the beat of drums before moving across the bay.
— **Kim-Mai Cutler "Not In Our Name Student Protest Military Action in Iraq"** *Daily Cal* Oct. 7, 2002

The year 1969 was also the year that People's Park and Ohlone Park and Greenway were founded, which still exist and are widely recognized as having "kicked off" the modern day Ecology Movement by gaining worldwide recognition of the need for parks and open space in crowded urban areas.
—**Matthew Artz "Miguel Altieri: Scientist Mourns Gill Tract's Demise"** *Berkeley Daily Planet* Oct. 28, 03

THE PEOPLE'S PARK in Berkeley in the new millennium resembles greatly the original, Edenic People's Park prior to its temporary fencing, occupation, and partial destruction by military and quasi-military forces unleashed on May 15, 1969. With its trees, expanse of lawn, and experimental and conventional gardens at the west end, the Park is a place of greenery and peacefulness in an urban area that lacks such charm.
—**Wendy Schlesinger "The Whole World is Watching"**

Zen & Now
I am the same
now as then
a work of Zen
a dancing sprite—
The Park.
—**Wendy Schlesinger, 2005**

And it is as a symbol that People's Park has always been most powerful; an icon for an age. But just as times have changed, so has the symbol. The path from 1969 to 1991 runs straight through People's Park. What has happened to the park reflects the evolution of our society.

When People's Park first was founded, it stood for the hope we felt then, the belief that everything was possible if we stood together, the knowledge that the best still lay ahead. People's Park is now a symbol for the despair of our time—the homeless people there a living statement of all we didn't achieve, the park a ragged reminder of those dashed dreams....The economic devastation of the Reagan presidency created a homeless problem that, in Berkeley, found its nexus in the park. As our social structure became more frayed, more and more tattered people took refuge there. So as our future becomes more precarious, the last thing we want to see are the homeless, the ghosts of America's Future....And how can students, most of whom weren't even born when the first battles for People's Park were fought--who can't even find Vietnam on the map—be expected to understand its historical importance?

For their ignorance, we can blame the same shoddy, uncaring society that turned People's Park into a de facto homeless shelter, the same society which has taught the students to hate the homeless.

What has happened at—and to—People's Park is simply a microcosm of the rest of our culture. What we have allowed to happen there tells us much about who we have become.
— **"Wither People's Park"** *East Bay Guardian* Sept. 1991

Display in Addison St. Windows
—*Brenda Prager, Nancy Delaney, Terri Compost*

**People's Park
20th Anniversary**

Part of my heart is buried in People's Park.
Leave it alone.
It's the part that will never be reasonable,
never grow up and know better
and do worse.
It's young;
breathing is sweet to it, and wild and scary.
It remembers meeting soldiers' bayonets with daffodils.
It remembers tear-gas drifting over swing sets.
It will always be young.
Leave it alone.
I go to the Park sometimes to talk to it.
Not often. Time passes
and it doesn't always recognize me.
But it tells me there are many hearts
buried with it.
All young, all proud of what they made
and fought for. Do not disturb them.
Do not build on them.
Do not explain that times have changed.
Do not tell them it's for their own good.
They've heard that before.
They will not believe you.
There are many hearts buried in People's Park
and a part of my own as well.
Oh, leave them alone.

—**Julia Vinograd, 1989**

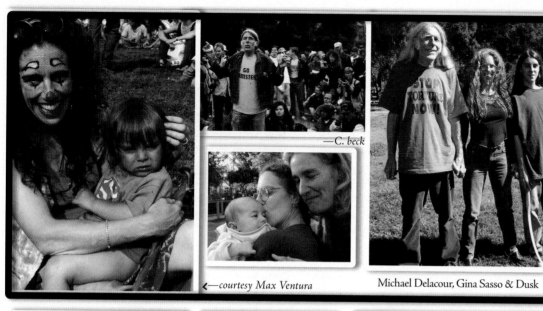

—C. beck

←courtesy Max Ventura

Michael Delacour, Gina Sasso & Dusk

—courtesy Wavy Gravy

—courtesy Wavy Gravy

Wavy Gravy supporting the Park over many years

—Brenda Prager

—courtesy Lisa Stephens

—Lydia Gans

—Allen Stross

Holding the Sacred Park Hoe, 2008

Ted Chenowith,
UC liaison with park gardeners, 1979

David Axelrod

Quinn and Elisa

176

The point is that the Park began to embody, not just the negation of capitalist principles of property and land-use, but some glimmering of the method and substance of a consciously visionary socialism rising from the ashes and the mud...Although the future of People's Park remains unclear, people have begun to look towards many ways of implementing the basic principles of the park: community, spontaneity, and opening of time, space and life in relation to the environment. **—John Oliver Simon, "The Meaning of People's Park"**

I fought before to defend the park and would do it again, though I hope that the time doesn't come soon. I don't want to spend all my time fighting. That feeling of struggle, everyone coming together against a common enemy, is so exciting. Looking back fondly on the struggle is so self-gratifying. But actually appreciating something good before it's gone is much harder.

—Aaron Cometbus, 1996

People's Park history is long and appears to be never ending.

—UCPD Berkeley History (police.berkeley.edu/ucpdhistory)

Imagine the park as an excellent location for open air fine arts shows, solar energy exhibitions, ethnic holiday celebrations and theatrical festivals. The university and the community could join hands to develop the park as an experimental cultural center-while respecting the original symbolic concept.

—Alice Blandy, *Daily Cal* **Feb. 12, 1985**

The hope that I nourish today is that the society will take up the challenge and enter into a process that will, as it goes on, enable us to transform our country by bringing to life the millions of the frustrated, the discarded, and the unused. I think that some part of that aspiration found expression in the spirit that went into People's Park. I think it may well be that in digging there they somehow uncovered the conscience of a city.

—Fred Cody, KPFA May 23, 1969

It is this lack of understanding that explains why students today see People's Park as an often frightening, always dingy place instead of a historical landmark. For me this park isn't merely a topic of debate, it's a piece of real estate I pass every day on my way to and from campus. I just wish the self-appointed guardians of the park would remove their circa 1969 rose-colored glasses and see the park for what it has become... I'm not sure what the next 30 years hold for People's Park but one thing is for certain: eventually, its fate will be in the hands of my generation.

—Tamara Keith, *Daily Cal* **April 14, 1999**

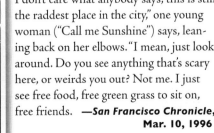

I don't care what anybody says, this is still the raddest place in the city," one young woman ("Call me Sunshine") says, leaning back on her elbows. "I mean, just look around. Do you see anything that's scary here, or weirds you out? Not me. I just see free food, free green grass to sit on, free friends. **—San Francisco Chronicle, Mar. 10, 1996**

And yet, there is still the strong pull of that Berkeley idealism. Would that one could distill it, and remove the impurities, and bottle it, and provide a mandatory daily dose for all our politicians, and businessmen, and journalists, and -- well -- all the rest of us.

— "A Grassy Park" www.narhist.ewu.edu

Today, it is one of the last remaining symbols of an era that in so many ways shaped the perceptions and values of our society. As a historical/educational resource, it has much to offer today's students and the students of tomorrow...People's Park can teach us how a local community can resolve its own needs and problems within a decentralized democratic structure. This model of direct public authority is often necessary for the needs and problems of a community to be recognized, and actualized. Since its creation in 1969, the park has encouraged community awareness of its needs and self-responsibility for their solution, using a public planning process in which decisions were made by and for the community of park users itself...By offering channels for individual participation in the planning and development of a community park, the social problems of apathy and alienation that plague our society can be replaced by a healthy enthusiasm for community oriented work. **—Dan Stotter, "A Case Study of Urban Ecology and Open Space"**

One of Lisa Stephen's dreams is to see the restoration of Derby Creek, the north fork of which, she says, once flowed through the south end of People's Park—right through where the volleyball courts now stand. Although Derby Creek was diverted into storm sewers when Berkeley was developed after the establishment of the university in the 1890's, Stephens says she can see the creek spontaneously re-emerging during rainy winters as a muddy area running diagonally across the park to the southwest. "It was probably an annual creek — running part of the year and dry the rest of the time. Some of it still flows through the park's soil."

—Rick DelVecchio, "Can People's Park change? Feelings are fierce on both sides about haven for homeless", SF Chronicle, June 26, 1993

People's Park remains a symbol of the free speech and anti-war era. On this small plot of land thousands of people over the years have "thrown their bodies on the gears of the odious military industrial machine". To many, like me, this victory beacons hope to continue the struggle for social justice and to restore our ravaged environment.
—**Dona Spring   www.peoplespark.org**

One of the items on the Berkeley College Republicans' agenda is that People's Park be bulldozed. "It was supposed to be a student dorm," says Kelso Barnett, a Berkeley College Republican... "How about calling it the 'Ronald Reagan Housing Center,'" Barnett quipped, adding, "that's not too likely." —*LA Times*, **April 27, 2003**

"When I came to Berkeley, People's Park seemed like a real symbol of freedom," said UC Berkeley student and Ukranian emigre Vladislav Kolegayev, 18, at Monday's (Landmarks Preservation) meeting. "It would be a terrible crime to remove people from the park, remove freedom from the park." —*Daily Cal*, **Nov. 8, 1995**

While the tension which attached such symbolism to the park has faded with time, the symbolism itself remains, and is at least as important to both the park's supporters and the park's detractors as the question of open space.
—**Wade Huntley, "PP: Past, Present and Future, The Symbolic Nature of the Park's Creation"**

A non-profit public Land Trust for People's Park Historic Community Open Space is currently being initiated and established in response to the legitimate needs and expressed will of many people. The single overriding objective of the Land Trust will be to preserve the People's Park site, near Telegraph Avenue in Berkeley, essentially as public parkland for the peaceful pleasure of the populace.
—**People's Park Press, "The Land Trust"**

We will be surprised if your intramural field is ever actualized unless it has the support of the people. We wonder at your lack of realism. The spirit that built People's Park is stronger than gas and cops. It is even stronger than universities. As followers of Jesus, we are committed to stand with that spirit, the spirit of the poor and alienated trying to create a new world on the vacant lots of the old.
—**Dick York from the Free Church of Berkeley, Sproul Plaza Rally May 15, 1969 "Battle for People's Park" Pacifica Tape Library**

Sometimes I think we are really the conservatives in this town. So reluctant to change, so steeped in tradition. As people come and go, especially young people, the park folks stick with it. As the rest of the city changes face and becomes a little more weary and cold, the park is still naive and welcoming. —**Aaron Cometbus, 1996**

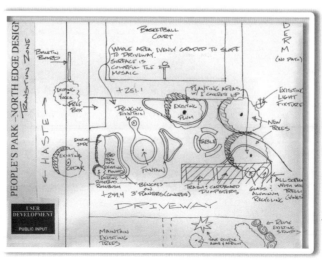

So I think they're going to continue and by hook or by crook they're going to try to build dorms on it, and eliminate it except for maybe a little patch for a memorial for some sell-out trip where they'll have "THIS IS THE MEMORIAL TO People's Park. IT WAS ONCE HERE." I think that that's what they want to do, and they will try, but I don't think it will succeed. —**John Delmos, nterviews by B.N Duncan, 93**

"I'm one of the hundreds of wounded veterans of the struggle for People's Park, twenty long years ago," said lawyer Mickey Tenenbaum. "This raggedy piece of land that we call People's Park is a vital and emotional piece of my personal history, and of the history and future of this community. If you try to take it back from us, don't think you can do it without a fight."...Councilmember Don Jelinek, who received a small bit of birdshot himself twenty years ago, charged that the university has actually forfeited ownership of the property by its neglect— a new twist on the theory of users' rights. "The university owes a blood debt to the city," he told the crowd. "The university just can't have People's Park. We have to develop it into the park we always intended it to be.".. "People's Park represented a dream for Berkeley," said BCA activist John Curl, "It represented the reconstruction of a better Berkeley and a better world, a better society.".....Three pro-park speakers gave up their time so a video could be shown, a condensed version of the documentary made by the Newsreel collective twenty years ago. First came a long and tedious stretch of ideological justification by Frank Bardacke, shifting uncomfortably from foot to foot in front of the People's Park fence. Then there were electrifying scenes of May 15, 1969: hippies with pickaxes, children playing in liberated territory, Dan Siegel exhorting the crowd to take the park, the march down Telegraph Avenue, then the streetfighting, the guns, police cars swerving crazily down Telegraph Avenue spewing gas....Then a funny thing happened. Across the years, on the garbled old soundtrack, the crowd could be heard chanting, "We want the park! We want the park!" Softly at first, then all together, the 1989 audience joined it: We want the park! We want the park!"
—**Paul Rauber, "Field of Dreams", *Express*, May 12, 1989**

People's Park has already been accorded official city landmark status as a historical open space. On any plaque erected on the site, please leave room for the names of those who will resist with their last ounce of devotion the decision to plant such a tombstone where once stood a tree. **—David Axelrod, *Daily Cal*, Dec. 1, 1987**

Please, do not let the University violate its word and our mutual agreement. Do not let the University again violate the Park. We must stand and fight united, every day and every generation, for every sacred inch of People's Park. Let 10,000 parks bloom!!! **—David Axelrod, April 24-25, 2006**

Imprisoned in concrete
People's Park is the deep wild heart
of the community called Berkeley.
It is where we go
To talk to the dead,
The lost, the unforgotten,
The unforgiven,
A place of crazy reconciliation
And ever deeper sanity,
Won, but not possessed.

Without the park
The city and the college would become
Just another society of brains for the machine.
But here, filtered by tree light,
We see how we can change
Where we can go
When there's nowhere else to go
How we must make
Blister after blister after blister
This world, at last, our home.
—Bill Bogert, April 25, 2009

You are the answer. The People's Park, a territorial and cultural battle which has cost two lives, belongs to you. Don't sell it out. Don't let UC or city money sway you. When they walk into the park to make "improvements", tell them they're violating the park's landmark status, a status which encompasses the user-developed traditions they wish to destroy. Just say, "UC out of the park." There aren't too many places where land was reclaimed from the rich for a shared purpose. This land belongs to you. **—Carol Denney, Slappsuit brochure 2006**

𝕿he University of California is in financial trouble and is beginning to sell off its property. The authors of this letter, who represent diverse interests in the Berkeley community, believe the City should expedite the purchase of People's Park from the University.

𝖂e, the undersigned, hope a transfer of ownership of the park will resolve a continuing debate over the Park's future.

Shattuck Avenue Merchants

Karen Adelman, manager Saul's Restaurant
Lori Ann, manager U.C. Copy
Ashraf, owner CopyWorld
Mohammad Bahrana, manager La Cascada
Karen Baughman, manager Ned's Warehouse
Rukhxie Bhumbla, manager Copy Central
Herbert Bibins, Black Oak Books
Charles Betz, Missing Link Bicycle Collective
Sarah Brand, Smokey Joe's Cafe
R. K. Brewer, manager McKevitt Used Cars
Michael Capperauld, owner UC Glass Company
Ruby Chan, owner Repro Express
Mona Chatal, Beads Plus
Teresa Clarke, director Northern Calif. Land Trust
April Davis, coordinator Homeless Action Center
Roger Dunn, owner Roger Dunn Printing
Peter Edinoff, owner Model Garage
Molly English, owner Camps and Cottages
Gerardo Franco, manager Shattuck Ave. Self Storage
Mansorr Ghanem, manager Brothers Liquors
Jeanie Gilmartin, manager Berkeley Florist
Betty Goto, manager Model Shoe Review
Alfonso Guerrero, owner Guerrero's
E. Hill, owner Istanbul Grill
Bonnie Hughes, the Art Gallery
Howard Hurwith, manager db Audio
Millicent Johnson, manager Berkeley Community Law Center
Stewart Johnston, manager Johnston Minicar
Martin Kanemoto, manager Thai Dishes
Lisa Kaufman, manager Baubles and Beads
Natalya Kougler, manager Lhasa Karnak Herb Co.
Kumar, manager Thai Express
La Pena Collective
Nanon Madison, owner The Phoenix Pastifico
N. K. Makam, owner Pro Per Publishing
Todd Malone, manager General Appliance
Dan Mayer, Ag Photo
Richard Mazzera, manager Chez Panisse
Ali Mirabdal, owner Cal Copy
Mehrdad Naima, owner Starry Plough
Ron Nilson, manager Berkeley Espresso
Lisa Onomoto, manager Comic Relief
Carol Jo Papac, manager Mephisto Shoes
Ali Parishan, manager Paris
Angela Pecot, owner Romantic Notions
Ella Peregrine, Homeopathic Educational Services
Bill Roxie, owner Roxie Deli
Bruce Schuitemaker, owner Shen Nong Herbs
Avinoash Sharma, manager Krishna Copy
Khalid Sheraga, owner Khyber Pass
Adam Smith, manager Juicy News

Telegraph Avenue Merchants

Ade T. Aro, owner The African Bookmark
Rigoberto Alonso, manager C'est Cafe
Jamail Ahmadzai, owner Nomad's Gallery
Kamal Ayyad, owner Fred's Market
Rebecca Baker, manager Tienda Ho
Phillip Barry, owner Shambhala Books
Thomas Bauer, manager Campus Textbook Exchange
Lynn Beckhusen, manager La Val's Pizza
Wayne Brougham, owner Cartesian Bookstore
Tracey Buck, manager Leopold Records
Scott Cambell, manager X-Large
Arthur Camball, owner Avant-Card
Daniel Choe, owner Steve's BBQ
Ken Chu, partner Quality Computer
Alan Dorsey, general manager TOGO'S
Omar Feralta, manager Fat Slice
Midori fernandez, manager Scissors
Monell Folsom, owner Continental Art Shop
Greg Guzaitis, manager The Gap
David Habibi, owner House of Kabab
Sung Han, manager Joy's
Augustine Hernandez, manager Eat A Pita
Jessie Hernandez, manager Urban Outfitters
Tom Hunt, the Reprint Mint
Ellie Javid, manager Maxi Hair
Allen Jones, owner Collectors Realm
Chris Juricich, manager Amous Vitamin Company
Claira Kennedy, manager Avant Card
Vinod Kumar, owner Krishna Copy
Kim, manager Narcissus
Sal Laser, manager la burrita
Allen Lewides, manager Amoeba Music
Andy Lester, manager Sharks
Marvin Lim, manager Blondie's
Kirk McKozak, manager Berkeley Basics
Alice Molloy, manager Mama Bears Bookstore
Morris Moskowitz, owner Moe's Books
Lauren Park, manager Wicked
Nancy Perez, manager Divali
Hatsjko Philogene, manager Sunshine Fashions
Gerald Prasad, manager Beeper City
Adnan Qadeer, manager Copy Vision
Ryan Rateaver, manager comics and Comix
Meghan Reek, manager Buffalo Exchange
Bob Reynoids, manager Presto Prints
Rebecca Rhine, Telegraph Ave. Merchants Association
Robyn Rodgers, manager Mars Merchantile
Guy Rose, manager Footlocker
Jay Sam, owner Cheese 'N Stuff
Ken Serachin, owner Rasputin's Records
Mohammad Shagasi, manager Zebra

DERBY CREEK

The north branch of Derby Creek historically flowed through what is now People's Park, and in the winter, it still does, in some fashion. There have been suggestions at various times to raise the creek. In 1998, at the request of the Community Advisory Board, a feasibility study was done by Wolfe Mason Associates.

—ed.

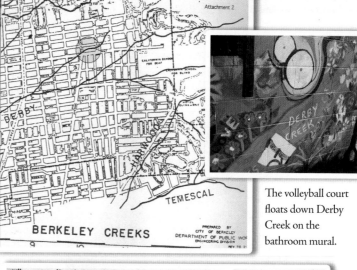

The volleyball court floats down Derby Creek on the bathroom mural.

Raise the Creek

PEOPLE'S PARK, CREEK CONCEPT LOOKING WEST.

Derby Creek Feasibility, People's Park. Creek Concept Looking West
Wolfe Mason Associates, Inc. 4.8.98

It would be wonderful to see what would happen if we restored Derby Creek, which has been underground for over 100 years. As an institution of higher learning with a motto of 'Let There Be Light,' UC should be interested. It would be a great experiment to see what kind of riparian landscape we could create around it, to see what kind of birdlife it would attract. But I think we're living in a time of limited vision.

—Lisa Stephens,
Downtown
(NYC), 1991

Derby Creek Feasibility, People's Park, Illustrative Plan,
Wolfe Mason Associates, Inc. 4.6.98

Marcus and KerryLiz

Tom and Jon L.

Michael Diehl

Danny and Katy

181

Juan Carlos Miller

—Jonathan Taylor photo

Al Haber and Odile

Frances Townes,
— Lydia Gans Photo

183

184

186

—*Roosevelt Stephens*

187

You?

Bibliography

http://www.peoplespark.org

"The Whole World is Watching", Harold Adler (Berkeley Art Center Association, Berkeley, 2001)

"Berkeley at War: The 1960s", W.J. Rorabaugh (Oxford University Press, N.Y., 1989)

"What Really Killed Rosebud?", Claire Burch (Regent Press, Berkeley, 2001) (includes a Park chronology 1957-97)

"People's Park of Berkeley: Then and Now", A Claire Burch Film (Regent Press, Berkeley, 2008)

"People's Park", Alan Copeland and Nikki Arai (Ballantine Books, N.Y., 1969)

"Protect the Earth", Thomas Parkinson (City Lights, San Francisco, 1970)

"The Right to the City: Social Justice and the Fight for Public Space", Don Mitchell (Gilford Press, NY, 2003)

"The Creation of the People's Park — A Love Story from a Leader's Point of View", Wendy M. Schlesinger (unpublished)

"Takin' it to the Streets: A Sixties Reader", Alexander Bloom, Wini Brieines (Oxford University Press, NY, 1995)

"That Patch of Ground ... called People's Park" (Berkeley, 1970)

"We Protest : A Photographic Study of the Bay Area Protest Movement, 1969", photographs by William Irwin ; foreword by William L. Ellis (Rip Off Press, San Francisco, 1970)

"Write on: Occasional Essays '65 - '85", David Lodge (Secker & Warburg, London, 1986)

"Cody's Books, The Life and Times of a Berkeley Bookstore, 1956 to 1977", Pat and Fred Cody (Chronicle Books, SF, 1992)

"The People's Park", Stanley Irwin Glick, (Dissertation State U of NY at Stony Brook, 1984)

"People's Park : the Rise and Fall(?) of a Religious Symbol", Gustav H. Schultz, (Manuscript, UC Bancroft Library, 1973)

"People's Park" [motion picture] (California Newsreel, 1969)

"Days of Blood- Nights of Terror" (Special Edition of the Daily Cal Berkeley, May 14- May 23, 1969)

"Green Flag", Sandra Corrie & Laura Stine, (City Lights, San Francisco, 1969)

"The People's Park Controversy : Chronology of Events, June 1967-May 30, 1969", (Academic Publishing , Berkeley)

"Negotiation Report", People's Park Negotiating Committee, (1969)

"Berkeley in the Sixties", documentary film, Mark Kitchell (1990)

"Dialectics of Confrontation: Who Ripped Off the Park?", Robert Scheer (Ramparts, 1969)

GREEN FLAG

PEOPLES PARK

No. 3 JOURNAL FOR THE PROTECTION OF ALL BEINGS , 1969

DO IT YOURSELF GARDENS & PARKS

Let 1000 Parks Bloom
The Earth Divided We Shall Make Whole,
So it Will Be a Common Treasury For All

Reclamation of abandoned urban lots and their creative transformation into life giving parks and gardens may be a crucial key to our survival. They can provide local food sources that do not require petroleum to transport, as well as animal habitat, educational opportunities, oxygen, beauty, and peace.

Steps to a Community Garden Space:

1. Gather community together. Involve locals, neighbors, youth, elders, homeless, parents, artists, schools...

2. Assess what already lives there; trees, weeds, animals, people...Work with the unique features of that location...water catchment off nearby buildings, natural swales, wetlands... Be aware of contamination, learn the history of your land, test the soil for lead and other toxins if you can. Use raised beds if needed. Attempt remediation with sunflowers, mustards, mushrooms, compost.

3. Plan the garden; fruit trees where they won't block the sun, garden paths, sitting areas, perennial beds, compost sites, water sources, swales to catch water on slopes, annual beds, greenhouse, tool box, chicken coop, ponds and wetlands, drier areas, bee hives... Research your projects and check out other gardens. Vision big, start small. Plant your fruit trees.

4. Use sledge hammers to break up concrete. Use rubble, broken concrete, logs from tree trimmers, whatever is available to make garden beds and paths. Use vertical space. Trellis walls. Consider rooftop and container gardens. Sheet mulch over large weedy areas with cardboard and organic matter (wood chips, compost, weeds). Start cultivating in a small area and work outward.

5. Recycle organic waste on site. Compost! Bring in restaurant, home and neighborhood food scraps, brewery waste, manure, dumpster finds, coffee grounds etc., mix with woodshop shavings, straw, leaves, garden waste, shredded newspapers. The right mix of Browns, Greens, Air and Water for good compost. Build and enrich your soil. Soil Health is Wealth! Use cover crops (fava beans) to enrich soil. Rotate crops.

6. Research planting schedules and plants that do well locally. Get seeds and starts from local nurseries, seed swaps, Seed Savers Exchange, other gardeners. Start baby plants inside, or on site. Save your own seeds! Keep notes. Learn, experiment. Select the best seed to adapt plants to your garden. Mulch! to save water, keep down weeds, and nourish the soil. Use cardboard, straw, compost, leaf litter, cocoa husks, natural fiber fabric..divert organic matter from the waste stream. Use wood chips on paths.

7. Eat weeds (chickweed, mallow, purslane, dandelion etc.) and pests (snails, aphids, grasshoppers...) Eat what is in abundance. Encourage natural predators. Encourage and appreciate diversity. Provide animal habitats. Enjoy.

Use your garden to share:
Food, clothes, tools, information, classes and announcements, stories, songs, childcare, Love.

Balance, Diversity, Wildness, Freedom, Life.

Parking Lots to Parks   Food Not Lawns
Believe Love   Free the Earth
Reclaim the Land for Life